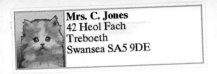

WHAT I

RATIONAL-EMOTIVE THERAPY?

A PERSONAL AND PRACTICAL GUIDE

BY

WINDY DRYDEN & JACK GORDON

Published by Gale Centre Publications for

THE GALE CENTRE, WHITAKERS WAY, LOUGHTON, ESSEX, IG10 1SQ. Tel (01) 508 9344.

Cover: Lizzie Spring. ISBN 1 870258 08 8 © W. Dryden & J. Gordon 1990.

Published by Gale Centre Publications

Whitakers Way

Loughton, Essex

IG10 1SQ

Printed in Great Britain by BPCC Wheatons Ltd, Exeter

British Library Cataloguing in Publication Data

Dryden, Windy

    What is Rational - Emotive Therapy?

    I. Title   II. Gordon, Jack, 1921 -

    616.8914

    ISBN 1 870258 08 8

CONTENTS

PREFACE

Why a personal and practical guide?

The personal and practical guides aim to help you understand what a particular therapy is about and what it feels like to experience it and to be a therapist in it. The check lists, descriptions, exercises and case histories in the guides are designed to allow you to form an individual study programme or a study programme with a group of colleagues. This programme will not turn you into therapists nor will it enable you to work on a deep level on therapeutic problems and it is not designed with either of these aims in mind. What it will do is give you an experience of how the therapeutic method works by suggesting practical exercises you can do yourself. It will also give you an experience of what it feels like to be a therapist giving that sort of therapy, the sort of problems for which the therapy can be used to help and the likely outcome.

After this study programme you will at the very least know what the therapy is about and be able to talk coherently about it. You will also have a better idea of whether you would want to be a client in that form of therapy and whether you would want to develop an expertise in it. I also hope that experienced and practising therapists will be able to find elements in the therapies described which they will be able to use to supplement and develop their own skills.

It is generally a requirement of training as a therapist that the therapist undertake therapy. It often strikes me as odd that therapists writing about their work make only scant references to their own therapy.

Therapists seem to be particularly reticent in talking about their own therapy, yet at the same time maintain that there is no stigma attached to therapy.

Therapy is not a science, it is an art and research has shown that the individual qualities of the therapist are often more significant than the method used. It seems odd that so little writing about therapy includes the personal experiences of therapists and their difficulties and failures in therapy.

The current Green revolution and the growth of interest in alternative therapies means that we are starting to pull away from the deification of scientific objectivity. This poses a problem for psychotherapy which has for so long been trying to gain acceptance by the scientific community. In its attempt to gain respectability and distance from the parodies of the actor and cartoonist, psychotherapy has used a form of scientific research and writing which alienates therapy from its true roots which are in the arts and the social sciences and not the natural sciences.

If, as I believe, psychotherapy is a search for an answer to that most fundamental of questions "Who am I", it is as much a search for a personal morality as a cure for mental pain and psychological disease. Then there is every place for subjectivity in the process itself and in books there is a place for the personal history and the personality of the author.

Humanistic psychology tends to provide more space for human error and fallibility on the part of the therapist but even in that discipline there is not enough trust for people to really be open about themselves. In this series I have made no attempt to edit out the personal approach of the authors, far less my own personality. In fact, I have encouraged them to include their personal experiences. There are plenty of books on every method of therapy written from the so called objective viewpoint and this series is offered as a counterweight to them.

The personal and practical guides do not take part in the internecine nor the intranecine battles that proliferate in most therapies but aim to put its readers in an informed position where they can make up their own mind. I welcome feedback from readers and as the books are printed on short runs can often incorporate it in future editions.

A note on Gender: to avoid the awkwardness of phrases like him/or, he/she the male authors of the series are asked to use the words he, him, etc. while the female authors use the female pronouns.

Derek Gale.

CHAPTER ONE

THE FINGER POINTING EXERCISE

When I *(WD)* run an introductory workshop on Rational-Emotive Therapy, I usually begin with an exercise that I call The Finger Pointing Exercise. I want you to imagine that you are attending the workshop as a participant and to monitor your reactions as I take you through the exercise.

"Think of a secret that you would not want anyone else to know about, not even your best friend. It's a secret - something of which you are ashamed. Your secret could involve an action that you feel particularly ashamed about, or it could be a personal weakness that you would not want anyone else to know about. Now, continue to think about it, because in a moment I am going to walk among you and I am going to point a finger at one of you. When I do that, I want the person concerned to go to the centre of the room. Then I am going to ask that person to disclose the secret in front of the rest of the group."

At this point in the exercise I walk round the circle in front of everybody with my pointed finger raised above my head, poised to point at the person I will single out to disclose his or her secret in public. I walk in front of all the workshop participants several times around the circle. But, I do not point at anybody! Instead, I say, "OK, I'm now going to ask you to share your feelings. What did you actually feel as I walked round and round in front of you, my finger poised in the air and about to point directly at any one of you - perhaps even you?"

What would **your** feelings have been if you had been sitting in that circle of workshop participants? Keep your feelings in mind as I am now going on to discuss some common emotional reactions that workshop participants have said they experienced in response to this exercise.

SOME EMOTIONAL REACTIONS TO THE FINGER POINTING EXERCISE

Quite a few participants have said that they experienced anxiety. Let me give you a couple of examples. One participant, Jock, said that his anxiety was related to the negative reactions that he anticipated he would receive from the rest of the group in response to disclosing his secret. On further exploration, Jock's anxiety was related to the following:

He predicted that the others in the group would consider him a bad person for doing such a "shameful act" in the past, However, this prediction was only part of the story. Jock not only had a preference that other people in the group would think well of him, but he was also demanding that they **must** approve of him. From this "must" he then concluded, "Because other people absolutely must approve of me, and I predict that they won't, then

(a) it would be **awful** if they thought badly of me,

(b) I couldn't stand it if they thought badly of me, and

(c) I would be a bad person if they thought that I was a bad person."

Freda, another workshop participant, also reported feeling anxious during the exercise. However, her anxiety was related to a different aspect of the situation. Freda believed that, if she was chosen to reveal her secret, she would have no choice but to do just that. Freda's belief was not only based on her desire to act in a cooperative manner in the group, but, in addition, she believed that she absolutely had to act cooperatively, even though she did not want to. Freda drew the following conclusions from this demand:

(a) that it would be terrible if she did not act in a cooperative manner,

(b) that she could not tolerate being non-cooperative, and

(c) that she would think less of herself if she did not cooperate by disclosing her secret.

Other participants reported feeling concerned, but not anxious. For example, Heather stated that she experienced concern during the exercise. Her feelings of concern stemmed from a preference, not a demand. Her preference was:

(a) "I don't really want to behave in this way but there's no reason why I must not decline Dryden's invitation to disclose my secret."

(b) "If I declined the invitation and other people in the group thought badly of me, that would be unfortunate, but not terrible."

(c) "It's uncomfortable to be disapproved of, but I can stand it. It's hardly unbearable." And

(d) "I can accept myself in spite of others' disapproval and not put myself down."

George also reported experiencing concern in this exercise. In this case George's concern was related to discomfort, and stemmed from his belief:

(a) " I prefer to be comfortable in workshop situations, but there is no reason why I have to experience comfort. Discomfort is just that, uncomfortable but not awful." And

(b) "I can put up with the discomfort and see what happens. There is no reason why I can't stand these feelings of discomfort."

Yet a further group of participants reported that they experienced anger in response to this exercise. Madeleine was one such participant. She considered that my behaviour was unbecoming of a workshop participant in that I was unfairly putting pressure on other people. However, her angry feelings did not stem from the presumed fact of my acting unfairly towards the group. Instead, Madeleine's anger was created by her demands, namely,

(a) that I, as a workshop leader, **must not** act unfairly,

(b) that it's scandalous and terrible that I do so,

(c) that she can hardly put up with my behaviour, and

(d) that I am something of a rotten person for acting in this manner.

In fact, this anger related to my "unfair behaviour" is a fairly common reaction among workshop participants.

However, other people reported feeling annoyed at my behaviour, rather than angry at me. Susan, for example, also considered that I was acting unfairly, but she did not demand that I must not do so. Her belief was related to a non-demanding desire. She reported her beliefs in this way:

(a) " I strongly prefer Dr Dryden not to act in this way but there is absolutely no reason why he must not do so."

(b) "It's too bad that he acts in this unfair manner but it isn't terrible."

(c) "He's a fallible human being for acting in what I consider to be a wrong manner, but he is not condemnable for it."

A minority of workshop participants reported positive feelings in response to this exercise. For example, Harriet's feelings were based on the hope that I would choose her to report on her secret in front of the group, because if I did that, it would give her the opportunity to practice her newly developed assertive skills. She was actually looking forward to saying, "No! I refuse to tell you my secret." Her feelings changed to disappointment when I didn't choose her, or indeed anybody.

Michael reported having feelings of pleasure in response to this exercise. He focussed on the fact that he was learning a good technique that he could use with his own students and that he was getting what he wanted from the workshop: new ideas.

Now, how did you feel? We'll come back to your reactions at the end of our discussion of this exercise.

THE PURPOSE OF THE FINGER POINTING EXERCISE

My aim in carrying out the Finger Pointing Exercise is to teach workshop participants that it is not the objective situation that people are in that makes them experience feelings. The emotional reactions that people experience in relation to events in their lives are created and maintained by both the interpretations they make about these events, and particularly, their beliefs and evaluations about these interpretations. Notice how some of the workshop participants focussed on "threatening" aspects of the situation. This was particularly true of those who experienced anxiety and concern. But, also note that these interpretations on their own did not discriminate between those who experienced anxiety and those who experienced concern. While interpretations that threat exists in a given situation limit people to experiencing anxiety or concern, the interpretation on its own does not account for the experience of either anxiety or concern. The deciding factor here is the evaluation that people make of their interpretations. Thus, those who experienced anxiety not only interpreted the given situation as threatening, they also evaluated it as "terrible", as a situation that **must not** exist and which they could not stand if it were to come about. Moreover, some of those experiencing anxiety would devalue themselves in certain circumstances were the threat to materialise.

It is important to note that those who experienced concern, rather than anxiety, during the exercise, also focussed on the possibility of threat arising from the exercise, but these people evaluated the threat in more flexible ways. In other words, they did not like the idea that the situation might be threatening, and they definitely preferred that a threatening situation would not arise; but - and this is the crucial point - they did not **demand** that a threatening situation absolutely must not exist.

Now, compare these reactions above with the feelings of anger which some participants reported they experienced during the Finger Pointing Exercise. Those people who felt angry tended to make interpretations about my behaviour, namely, that I was acting in an unfair manner. This interpretation influenced them to experience either anger or annoyance, but as in the preceding example of anxiety or concern, this interpretation on its own was not the deciding factor in determining which emotional reaction would predominate. Once again, it was these participants' belief or evaluation that was linked to the interpretation that decided the emotional outcome. Thus, participants who **demanded** that I must not act unfairly tended to experience anger, while those other participants who merely preferred that I did not act unfairly, but refrained from escalating their preference to a **demand** that I must not act unfairly, tended to experience annoyance or displeasure.

Of those other workshop participants who experienced positive feelings of pleasure, note that their feelings were linked to interpretations that centred on the fulfillment of some desire. These participants were getting what they wanted; the exercise was, in some way, fulfilling their desires of what they wanted to get out of the workshop.

Now, what were your experiences while you attended in your imagination as a participant in this workshop exercise? Did you experience anxiety? Or was it merely concern? What, if any, threatening interpretation were you placing on the reality of my walking around with my finger pointed in the air, ready to single someone out to expose a personal secret in front of the group? If anxiety was your predominant feeling, look for the demands you were making in your head about this threat. Look, until you find, exaggerated evaluations such as, "It's awful, I can't stand it!" Were you devaluing yourself in your mind if the aspects you found personally threatening in the situation were to come true?

If concern, not anxiety, was your predominating feeling, identify your non-dogmatic preferences about the threat occuring. They will be found to be of the order: "It's unfortunate if what I fear actually comes about, but it isn't terrible. "Terrible" is a figment of my imagination. If others in the group disapprove of me and consider me weak for feeling afraid and showing concern, that is unfortunate, but I can still accept myself in the face of their criticism."

Did you experience feelings of anger or annoyance? Once again look for the interpretations you made concerning my behaviour. Did you regard it as unfair? Was I transgressing some rule or standard that you held concerning appropriate leader behaviour in workshop situations? If you felt angry, what demands were you making in your head about me? For example, were you demanding that I **must not** act in the manner that I was acting? Were you telling yourself that it was terrible that I was acting in this manner? Did you believe that you couldn't tolerate this deplorable situation? And what sentences were you turning over in your mind to devalue me on account of my "terrible" behaviour?

If you felt annoyed or displeased rather than angry or enraged, look for the beliefs that stemmed from your preferences rather than your musts. Were you, for example, wishing or preferring that I would act differently but not demanding that I absolutely must act differently? Did you convince yourself that it may have been bad that I was acting in this way, but that it was hardly terrible or catastrophic, and that you could tolerate the situation and accept me as a person who was making an error without, in any way, putting me down as a human for making an error?

If you experienced positive feelings, which of your desires were being met during your imagined participation in the exercise? You may be interested to know that whenever I have carried out this exercise I have never actually asked anybody to come out into the centre of the group and disclose their "secret" to the other workshop participants. I also tell the group that this is the only time during the workshop that I will intentionally act in a manner designed to conceal my true purpose. Remember that my purpose is to show the group that people have emotional reactions to their interpretations **and** their evaluations of situations, and not to the situations themselves. Interpretations influence people in the kind of emotional reactions they are likely to experience, but they do not of themselves determine which particular emotion they will experience. Rather, it is the evaluative beliefs that people hold about events and their interpretations of events that are the most important determinant of the way people feel.

CHAPTER TWO

THREE MORE EXPERIENTIAL EXERCISES

IDENTIFYING FEELINGS OF HURT AND DISAPPOINTMENT

In this exercise we want you to imagine a time when you felt very hurt about something that someone close to you had done. Vividly imagine the behaviour of the other person and really get in touch with your feelings of hurt. Now, see if you can identify the beliefs that you had at the time that underpinned your feelings of hurt. In particular, look for the demands that you were making about the other person. For example, were you demanding that the other person must not behave in the way that he or she did, particularly if the other person was a loved one or family member who ideally should not have treated you in the manner that they did? Were you demanding that because you didn't deserve to be treated in this way, therefore the other person absolutely must not treat you in this way?

Let's assume you have identified those demands with which you eventually made yourself feel hurt. You start off with making demands. Now, what conclusions follow these demands? The conclusions, the evaluations you relate to your demands are the determinants of your hurt. What kind of evaluations? Well, were you, for example, telling yourself that it's terrible or horrible that the other person acted in this betraying manner towards you? Were you telling yourself that you can't stand the other person's behaviour and that he or she was a rotten person for behaving in the way they did? Perhaps you were feeling sorry for yourself: "Poor me! What a rotten world this is for allowing such behaviour to go on!"

Here, you will note that feelings of self-pity are often present when you feel hurt. Honestly look for these feelings and acknowledge that they exist when they are present. Ask yourself whether you were in any way putting yourself down. For example, were you convincing yourself that because the other person had treated you badly in a way you previously thought you didn't deserve, perhaps they were right after all and that you really were an undeserving, worthless person?

In the original Finger Pointing Exercise, you will recall that I *(WD)* made the point that in RET we distinguish between two types of negative emotions (e.g. anxiety versus concern, anger versus annoyance). As will be discussed later, feelings like anger and anxiety are regarded in RET as inappropriate negative emotions in that they tend to lead to self-defeating and other unwanted consequences, whereas feelings of concern and annoyance are seen as appropriate negative emotions because they help the individual to adjust and to cope more effectively with negative life events. Feelings of hurt are regarded in RET as inappropriate negative emotions because they also frequently lead to self-defeating outcomes as well as doing little to improve personal relationships. It is a common experience that people who feel hurt often withdraw from the other person in a kind of sulking hostility. The constructive alternative to "hurt" is "disappointment". Now, try this exercise in disappointment.

Close your eyes and vividly imagine another time in your life when another person whom you were close to, treated you badly or inconsiderately and unfairly. Or you could have been betrayed as described in the exercise on hurt. This time, however, choose an example where you felt disappointed, rather than hurt, about the experience. Try to choose an example that was as serious as the example you chose when doing the exercise on hurt, but one to which you responded with disappointment rather than with hurt. Close your eyes and vividly imagine that circumstance. See the person acting in the way that they did, and relive those feelings of disappointment you experienced at the time. Right, now let's see if we can distinguish between the beliefs that underpin hurt and the beliefs that underpin disappointment.

While you are re-living your feelings of disappointment, look for your non-dogmatic beliefs. These will take the form of desires, even strong desires or preferences that the other person had acted differently, but however desirable that might have been, there was no reason why they absolutely had to have acted any differently from the way they indubitably did act. If you found traces of demandingness, for example, demands that the other person must not have treated you in the way they did treat you, the chances are you are experiencing hurt, rather than disappointment. In that case, search your mind again for an example where your response was strong disappointment, and once you have found it, actively look for your non-demanding preferences.

Next, look for the conclusions that you came to following your non-demanding preference(s). Typically, these will be evaluative statements such as:

(a) "It's unfortunate that the other person acted in this way, but it's not terrible or catastrophic. I can definitely stand it although I'll never like it.

(b) Just because the other person is acting in such a bad manner, that doesn't mean that he or she is a good-for-nothing, or that the world is a rotten place for allowing such things to happen. I'm not a poor unfortunate soul who is being treated in a terrible manner, but simply a person who is not being treated as I think I deserve to be, or would like to be treated. Tough! There's no reason why I have to get what I think I deserve.

(c) I can still accept myself in the face of the other person's poor behaviour. Just because the other person is acting badly towards me that doesn't mean anything about me as a person in my own eyes.

(d) I can openly discuss with the other person the reasons for their poor behaviour while still accepting myself and in no way downing myself for being treated unfairly or inconsiderately."

How did you fare in these two exercises? If you've been successful you will see that in both feelings of hurt and disappointment, there are similar interpretations involved. These interpretations or inferences are that some other person has acted towards you in an unfair or betraying manner. However, what gives the experience of hurt on the one hand, and disappointment on the other hand their distinctive character, are the different beliefs involved. We have suggested that hurt is based upon a demanding attitude, that the other person must not act in the way they did, whereas in disappointment the belief is a more flexible one; in disappointment, you prefer, you wish that the other person did not act in such a bad manner, but you do not demand that they act differently from the way that they did act.

In addition, the conclusions you draw from these beliefs are different. In hurt, there are the conclusions that "it's terrible, I can't stand it, and the world is no good for allowing such conditions to exist." Also, you are probably telling yourself that you are diminished, or less worthy as a person as a result of such treatment being meted out to you.

By contrast, when you experience disappointment, and refrain from escalating your feelings to those of hurt, your conclusions are of the form:

(a) It is unfortunate, but hardly terrible that I am being treated in this way, but I can stand what I don't like and the world is hardly a rotten place just because such unfortunate behaviour takes place.

(b) I'm, certainly not a person to be pitied, either by myself or others, nor will I put myself down in response to the other person's poor behaviour towards me.

IDENTIFYING FEELINGS OF GUILT AND REGRET

This exercise is similar to the one above, but here you will be asked to identify an occasion when you felt guilty and a time when you felt regretful about breaking your own moral code. Before we begin the exercise we want to make the following point about the word "guilt". In RET, guilt is commonly used to mean feelings of guilt as distinct from guilty acts. You may be guilty of committing some misdeed, for example, but your feelings about the act are not the same thing as the act itself. Feelings of guilt are regarded as self-defeating and unhelpful or even harmful for reasons which will become obvious later.

First, remember a time when you felt very, very guilty about breaking your own moral code. The transgression of your code may have been related to something that you did (act of commission), or something that you failed to do (act of omission). Vividly picture in your mind your violation of your own moral code and stick with the feelings of guilt even though they are likely to be quite painful.

Now, while still remaining with your feelings of guilt see if you can identify the beliefs that underpin those feelings. For example, look for the demands that you made upon yourself. Were you telling yourself not only do I prefer to adhere to my moral code, but I absolutely must not break it under any circumstances? If you find such a belief, look for the conclusions you drew from this belief. Search for statements such as:

(a) "It's awful that I broke my moral code,

(b) I can't stand my behaving like that, and

(c) I'm a damnable, rotten person for doing so and less worthy in my own eyes than if I hadn't acted in this immoral manner."

Now, let's move on to the second step of this exercise, which is identifying feelings of regret. This time, think of an occasion when you once again broke your moral code and try to make it as serious a breach as the one you identified in the first part of this exercise on guilt. This time, however, choose a violation to which you responded with regret, rather than guilt. Vividly imagine yourself breaking your moral code and really get in touch with your feelings of regret. Once you have done this, look for the rational beliefs that underlay your feelings of regret. Look for statements like:

(a) "I really dislike breaking my moral code, but there's no reason why I absolutely must not break it.

(b) It's very unfortunate that I broke my moral code on this occasion, but it isn't terrible.

(c) This situation is bearable even though I admit it is most unfortunate, and

(d) I can accept myself as a fallible human being who did the wrong thing, and maybe I can learn something from my failure and possibly make amends, but I am not a rotten or less worthy person for having acted in such a bad way."

By now, you may see that while guilt and regret share the same interpretation of events, that is, that the person concerned has broken his or her moral code, the two feelings can be discriminated by differences in the kind of evaluative beliefs that the person makes about such an interpretation. In guilt, the evaluations are absolutistic and dogmatic; in regret they are more flexible and relative, more reality based.

EXERCISE ON PROCRASTINATION AND TAKING EFFECTIVE ACTION

In this exercise we want to help you to distinguish between the beliefs that underpin procrastination and those that underpin taking effective action. First, procrastination. While there are different kinds of procrastination, we want you to select an example where you put off doing something that was tedious but would have benefited you in the long run had you tackled the task at the time it arose. Let's assume that putting off this task was really self-defeating. But don't choose an example where you procrastinated because you were scared that if you did the task poorly you would condemm yourself for it. Take an example where the task was tedious but not threatening to your sense of self. Close your eyes and vividly imagine you are faced with the choice of doing, or not doing, this particular task. See yourself procrastinating. Stay with that scene for a couple of minutes.

Let's see, now, if you can identify the implicit beliefs that drove you to procrastination. First of all, how would you have felt initially if you had done the tedious task. It is likely that your predictions about your feelings would have centred on experiences of discomfort. OK, now look for the demands that you made about these feelings of discomfort. When you find them, you will probably identify beliefs such as:

(a) "I must not be uncomfortable. It's terrible to do something that I really don't want to do, or feel like doing.

(b) I can't stand personal discomfort, and

(c) The world is a rotten, unfair place for giving me more discomfort than I should have. I don't deserve to have a difficult life."

Now, once again, think of a time similar to the first when you were faced with a tedious task that you knew would pay you to tackle promptly, rather than be put off to a time when you might feel more like tackling it. Make this example a time when you actually did the task promptly, and that the consequences of not doing it would have been the same as in the previous example you chose. Now, close your eyes and vividly picture yourself doing the tedious task. How did you get yourself to do it? Once again, in RET we hold that the distinction lies in the type of beliefs that underpins these two different kinds of actions. If you look for these beliefs you will find statements of desire or preference, along the lines of:

(a) "I don't want to do this task, it's a real pain in the neck, but there's no reason why I must not do it now, and it would be better for me in the long term if I do buckle down and get cracking on it now; so I will.

(b) While it's too bad that this task is tedious, it's not terrible and I can definitely stand doing what I don't like. Tough!

(c) The world is neither good nor bad because I'm faced with tedious tasks, it just is the way it is."

In both these situations, the person is faced with a tedious task, and in each of them there are equally serious negative consequences for procrastinating behaviour. However, the distinction lies once again in the type of belief the person holds about the situation. Bear in mind that in procrastination the person doesn't experience immediate discomfort for putting off the disagreeable task. The procrastination protects you from the "pain" of doing the task there and then, but it generally makes things more difficult for you later, and most of the time you know that. Nevertheless, the beliefs you have about discomfort are implicit in accounting for your behaviour.

CHAPTER THREE

BASIC THEORETICAL IDEAS

Rational-Emotive Therapy is a theory of personality and a method of psychotherapy originated and developed by Albert Ellis, a clinical psychologist, in the 1950's. Ellis originally worked as a psychoanalyst, but became dissatisfied with psychoanalysis because it was, in his words, "inefficient", time-consuming and it did not produce very effective results. After experimenting with briefer forms of psychoanalytic forms of psychotherapy, Ellis was influenced by his longstanding interest in philosophy, particularly proponents of the Stoic school, of whom Epictetus is a good example. Epictetus stated that "men are disturbed, not by things, but by their views of things." Through his famous *Meditations,* the Roman emperor, Marcus Aurelius, publicized Stoic philosophy, and later philosophers such as Spinoza and Bertrand Russell helped to bring these views to the attention of the western world. It has been said that there is nothing new under the sun. This is partly true, in that everything has evolved from, or been constructed from, some antecedent or combination of antecedents. What is new is the coherent development of a philosophy and a set of psychological constructs into a workable and effective form of psychotherapy.

To emphasise the cognitive aspects of his therapy, and the methods of logical disputation derived from them, Ellis termed his new therapy "Rational Therapy". This was later changed to its present-day title, "Rational-Emotive Therapy", which is a more accurate description of the therapy because RET emphasises that cognition (or thinking), feeling and behaviour all inter-related and interacting processes which all have to be taken into account if treatment methods are to be effective. This point was stressed in Ellis's first major book on RET, entitled *Reason and Emotion in Psychotherapy* (Ellis, 1962).

GOALS, PURPOSES AND RATIONALITY

According to rational-emotive theory humans are happiest when we set up important life goals and purposes and actively strive to achieve these. In doing so, we had better acknowledge that we live in a social world and we are thus encouraged to develop a philosophy of enlightened self interest, which means pursuing our own valued goals while demonstrating what Alfred Adler called social interest - a commitment to helping others achieve their valued goals and a commitment to making the world a socially and environmentally better place in which to live. Given that we will tend to be goal directed, rational in RET theory means "that which helps people to achieve their basic goals and purposes whereas irrational means that which prevents them from achieving these goals and purposes" (Dryden, 1984, page 238). While rationality is not defined in any absolute sense, it does have three major criteria, (a) pragmatic, (b) logical and (c) reality based. Thus, a more extended definition of rationality would be that which helps us to achieve our basic goals and purposes, that which is logical (non absolutist) and that which is empirically consistent with reality. Conversely, irrationality means that which prevents us from achieving our basic goals and purposes, that which is illogical (especially, dogmatic and musturbatory) and that which is empirically inconsistent with reality.

RESPONSIBLE LONG RANGE HEDONISM

Rational-Emotive Therapy argues that humans are basically hedonistic in the sense that we seek to stay alive and to achieve a reasonable degree of happiness. Most people, also, wish to relate intimately with a few selected individuals of the same and/or the other sex. Rather than pointing to "pleasures of the flesh", hedonism in RET involves the concept of personal meaning. A person may be said to be acting hedonistically when she is happy acting in a manner which is personally meaningful for her. The concept of responsible hedonism means that we are advised to again be mindful of the fact that we live in a social world, and that ideally, our personally meaningful activities should not gratuitously harm other individuals or the world we share, but, if possible, help to make that shared world a better place to live in for ourselves and others.

RET makes an important distinction between short-range and long- range hedonism. We, RET maintains, are likely to be at our happiest when we achieve both our short-term and our long-term goals. However, we frequently defeat our best interests by going for short-term satisfaction even when we acknowledge that doing so will sabotage our gaining more worthwhile objectives in the longer term. For example, some people will knowingly risk putting their health in jeopardy in later years for the sake of enjoying an excessive consumption of some pleasant tasting but potentially harmful beverage. Many people strive to avoid discomfort in the present or immediate future even when it would be highly advisable to put up with the threatened discomfort in order to avoid an even greater and more prolonged discomfort later. A surgical operation may be put off because of the immediate discomfort it would entail; but if the outcome is an even more serious operation made necessary later on because of a worsening health condition, the consequence is a higher degree of pain and discomfort than if the lesser discomfort had been faced in the first place. In many similar ways, we sabotage our own best interests and block the realisation of our goals through our insistence on being comfortable, or at least, avoiding pain in the here and now. RET therapists encourage their clients to achieve a thought-out, realistic balance between the pursuit of their short-term and their long- term goals, while being mindful of the fact that what represents a healthy balance for one person, may be just the opposite for another person. Each person is best able to make that decision herself or himself once the counsellor has drawn up and explained the hedonic calculus or balance sheet.

ENLIGHTENED SELF-INTEREST

Enlightened self-interest means that we pursue our goals and strive primarily for our own happiness while being mindful that others have an equal right to strive for what they regard as significant in their lives. If we cynically disregard the rights of others to pursue their own paths to happiness, such antisocial conduct may well backfire with unfortunate results for everyone. We are advised to treat other people properly, with due concern for their rights, part-

e want to be, in our turn, treated properly by others and partly be-
cau.... int to help create the kind of world it is safe and beneficial for us to
live in. Morality, when it is rational, is not based on self- sacrificing, but on self-
interested motives. RET does not say that self-sacrifice is never justifiable.
There can be circumstances where an individual may, for a time, legitimately
put the interests of others, especially close loved ones, before his or her own interests, if the individual finds personal meaning and happiness in doing so. However, when putting the interests of others first becomes overwhelming and
apparently without some end in sight, RET would hold that such self-sacrific-
ing conduct is probably irrational in that it may not only be self-defeating, but
may also subtly harm the person receiving such attention. Clearly, enlightened
self-interest includes social interest. We live in a social world and would do well
to remember that human happiness is maximised under favourable social and
environmental conditions.

PHILOSOPHIC AND SCIENTIFIC EMPHASIS

Rational-emotive theory agrees with the ideas of George Kelly (1955) that
we are scientists and are able to appreciate that our philosophies are basically
hypotheses about ourselves, other people and the world around us, which need
to be tested. This is best accomplished in conjunction with our philosophical
abilities, particularly our ability to think critically about the logical and illogical
aspects of our thought. However, rational-emotive theory stresses that we are
born philosophers as well as scientists. We have the ability to think about our
thinking and to realise that we are highly influenced by our own implicit philosophies of life. These philosophies tend to be either relatively flexible and un-
dogmatic, or musturbatory and absolutist. Ellis maintains that while we have a
strong tendency, partly biologically based, to think and act irrationally, we also
have the ability to think critically about our own thinking and to judge whether
or not our hypotheses are consistent with perceived reality.

HUMANISTIC OUTLOOK

RET is not only philosophical and scientific in orientation, but it takes a specific humanistic-existential approach to human problems and their solution. This view conceptualises humans as holistic and indivisible, goal-directed organisms who have importance in the world just because we are human and alive, and who have the right to continue to exist and to enjoy and fulfill ourselves. It emphasises the ability of humans to create and direct our own destinies, and it encourages humans to unconditionally accept ourselves with our limitations while at the same time encouraging us to work towards minimising our limitations. RET agrees with the position of ethical humanism which "encourages people to live by rules emphasising human interests over the interests of inanimate nature, of lower animals or of any assumed natural order of deity". (Ellis, 1980, page 327.) However, this does not mean being ecologically or environmentally insensitive, or advocating the mindless slaughter of animals. And while we may disagree with others' religious views, we nevertheless uphold their right to hold their religious views. This outlook acknowledges people as human and in no way as superhuman or subhuman.

TWO BASIC BIOLOGICAL-BASED TENDENCIES

Rational-emotive theory hypothesises that we have a biologically-based tendency to think irrationally and a similar tendency to think rationally. It thus differs from other approaches to therapy in emphasising the power of these biologically-based tendencies over the power of environmental conditions to affect human happiness, although it by no means neglects the contribution of these environmental conditions to influence human emotion and behaviour. The view that irrational thinking is largely determined by biological factors, although always interacting with influential environmental conditions, rests on the seeming ease with which we think crookedly and the prevalence of such thinking even among those of us who have been rationally raised. Ellis has noted in this regard that "even if everybody had had the most rational upbringing, virtually all humans would often irrationally escalate their individual and social preferences into absolutistic demands on (a) themselves (b) other people and (c) the universe around them" (Ellis, 1984, page 20).[1]

Rational-emotive theory states, however, that we have a second biological tendency and that is to think rationally and to work towards changing our irrational thinking. Thus we have the ability to identify our irrational thinking, to realise why it is irrational and to change it to a more rational version and to continually work towards minimising, although certainly not eradicating, the impact of our tendency to think irrationally.

TWO MAJOR CATEGORIES OF HUMAN DISTURBANCES

Ellis has noted that human psychological problems may be loosely divided into two major categories, (a) ego disturbance and (b) discomfort disturbance. Ego disturbance relates to the demands that we make of ourselves and the consequent negative self-ratings that we make about ourselves when we fail to live up to our self-imposed demands. Furthermore, ego disturbance issues may underpin what at first glance may appear to be us making demands upon others or life conditions. For example, I may be angry at you because you are acting in a way which I perceive to be a threat to my "self-esteem". The fact that my anger is directed outwardly towards you seemingly serves to protect my own "shaky self-esteem". For a fuller discussion of this type of anger, the reader is referred to chapter eight.

Discomfort disturbance, on the other hand, seems much more related to the issue of human comfort. While the person may make demands about self, others and life conditions, the main issue in discomfort disturbance relates to dogmatic commands that comfort and comfortable life conditions must exist. As will be shown later, the healthy alternative to ego disturbance rests on a fundamental attitude of unconditional self-acceptance. This implies that we fully accept ourselves as human and essentially unrateable. The healthy alternative to discomfort disturbance rests on a philosophy of attaining a high level of frustration tolerance, or discomfort tolerance whereby we are prepared to tolerate

---

1   For a full discussion of Ellis's arguments concerning the biological basis of irrationality
     see Ellis (1976).

frustration of discomfort, not for the sake of it, but as a way o
stacles to our long-term happiness. In other words, when unple
are, for a time, unavoidable, it is better to put up with these unc
ditions while preparing oneself to change them in some constructive manner
later, rather than getting all hot and bothered about the situation and thereby
giving oneself two problems to deal with instead of only one.

THE THREE MAJOR MUSTS

Ellis originally identified 12 irrational ideas which from clinical observation he considered to be at the root of most emotional disturbance (for a full
discussion of these core irrational ideas, the reader is advised to consult Ellis,
1962). Most people appear to believe several unrealistic ideas with unhappy results in terms of their emotions and behaviours. All of them consist of some
form of absolutism - of unqualified demands and needs, instead of preferences
or desires. There are virtually innumerable expressed variations of these core
irrational beliefs but they all amount to the same thing in terms of their meaning.
In fact, these 12 or so supreme dictates that people impose on themselves can
be "collapsed" down to three main dictates that cause immense difficulties.
You've heard of the "Holy Trinity". Well, ours is the unholy or "Irrational
Trinity"!

The first dictate is:

(1) "Because it would be highly preferable if I were outstandingly compe-
tent and/or loved, I absolutely should and must be; it's awful when I am
not, and I am therefore a worthless individual."

The second irrational and unprovable idea is:

(2) "Because it is highly desirable that others treat me considerately and
fairly, they absolutely should and must, and they are rotten people who
deserve to be utterly damned when they do not."

The third impossible dictate is:

3) "Because it is preferable that I experience pleasure rather than pain,
the world absolutely should arrange this and life is horrible, and I can't
bear it when the world doesn't."

These three core irrational ideas and their various corollaries and sub-headings constitute the main factors in what we term neurosis or emotional/behavioural malfunctioning. And this implies that unless clients are shown how to recognise and uproot their irrational belief systems and replace them with sounder, reality-orientated philosophies, they are unlikely to surrender their self-defeating ways of relating to themselves and the world, and eventually to learn positive self-helping approaches to life.

In RET we maintain that if one is an empiricist and invents no absolute necessities or imperatives, it is almost impossible to become emotionally disturbed. Of course, you may still feel sad, or annoyed when faced with the inevitable, unfortunate aspects of living in the world. And when life goes well for you, you may feel joyful, or even ecstatic, "over the moon" as they say. "Rational" in RET does not mean unemotional. Rather, the more determined you are to be self-accepting, hedonistic and what Maslow termed self-actualising, by using your head and other faculties, the more emotional and in touch with your feelings you will tend to be.

THE 3 X 2 DISTURBANCE MATRIX

It is possible to take the three basic "musts" and the two fundamental categories of human emotional disturbance to form a 3 x 2 disturbance matrix (see Figure 1). The reader will recall that the three basic musts are, in their simplest form: I must; you must; life conditions must, and that the two fundamental categories of emotional disturbance are: Ego Disturbance (or Ego Anxiety); and Discomfort Disturbance (or Discomfort Anxiety).

Figure 1 : The 3 x 2 Disturbance Matrix

	Ego	Discomfort
I must	A	B
You must	C	D
Life must	E	F

(A) Ego Disturbance - Demands about Self

In this type of disturbance, it is quite clear that the person concerned is making demands upon herself and the main issue is her attitude towards herself. The major derivative from the "must" is some aspect of self-damnation, for example:

(a) "I must do well in my exams; I must obtain my degree, and if I don't, I'm no good."

Also, an equivalent demand is:

(b) "I must be loved and approved by certain people in my life, and if I'm not, that proves I'm no good."

(B) Discomfort Disturbance - Demands about Self

Here, the person makes demands about herself, but the real issue concerns her attitude towards discomfort. For example, "I must obtain my degree, because if I don't, I might have to settle for some kind of tedious manual job and my life conditions would be terrible and I couldn't stand that."

(C) Ego Disturbance - Demands about Others

In this example, the person is making demands about the way another person must, or must not act, but the real issue centres round her attitude towards herself. This often occurs when the person is angry about somebody and takes the form of a demand that the other person must not act in a certain way, because that way involves what the angry person perceives as a threat to her own self-esteem. For example, "You must treat me nicely because if you don't, that proves that you don't think much of me, and that means that I am no longer good."

(D) Discomfort Disturbance - Demands about others

Here, the person is making demands upon others, but the real issue concerns the realm of discomfort. For example, "You must treat me nicely and look after me because I couldn't stand the hard life I'd be faced with if you do not."

(E) Ego Disturbance - Demands about Life Conditions

On the surface, the person is making demands about some aspects of life conditions, but the real issue concerns her real attitude towards herself. As an example, "Life conditions under which I live must be easy for me, because if they are not then that's just proof of my own worthlessness."

(F) Discomfort Disturbance - Demands about Life Conditions

In this kind of disturbance we are dealing with a more impersonal from of low frustration tolerance. This type of discomfort is frequently seen when people lose their temper with inanimate objects, or in situations requiring a fair amount of patience. For example, "My car absolutely must not break down when I'm just about to use it, because I could not stand the frustration if it did." Or, "When I join a queue for some service, I must be served quickly because I can't stand delays in getting what I want."

PSYCHOLOGICAL INTERACTIONISM

Rational-emotive theory states that a person's thoughts, emotions and actions cannot be treated seperately from one another. Rather, they are best conceptualised as being overlapping or interacting psychological processes. This is the principle of psychological interactionism. So, for example, when I think about something, I also tend to have an emotional reaction towards it and also a tendency to act towards it in some way. Equally, if I have a feeling about some person then I am likely to have some thoughts about that person, and also again, a tendency to act in a relation to that person in a certain manner. Similarly, if I act in a certain manner towards some person or object, my action is based on the way I think and feel about that person or object.

RET is the best known for the emphasis it places on cognition, and for its cognitive restructuring components. While it is true that RET does emphasise the power of cognition to influence human happiness and disturbance, it fully acknowledges the affective and behavioural aspects and maintains that these fundamental human psychological processes almost always interact, and often in complex ways. Similarly, in this approach to psychotherapy, while cognitive restructuring methods are very important, they are by no means the sole methods in the therapeutic armamentarium. Rational-emotive therapists frequently use emotive, evocative and behavioural methods to encourage clients to change their thinking and acquire a more rational outlook on themselves and the world. RET therapists are seldom just interested in promoting symptom-removal. Instead, the therapist aims to help the client to examine and change some of his or her most basic values, particularly those values which have caused the client trouble in the past, and are likely to make the client disturbance-prone in the future. For example, if a client has a serious fear of failing on his job, the RET therapist would not merely help him or her to overcome that particular fear, and to be less afraid in future of failing vocationally. Instead, the client would be helped to give up all exaggerated fears of failing at **anything** and shown how to **generally** minimise their basic awfulising tendencies. It is a characteristic of RET that the usual goal of therapy is not only to eliminate the client's presenting symptoms, but to rid the client of many other non-reported symptom-creating propensities. In short, RET strives for the most elegant solution possible to the problem of emotional disturbance and is seldom content with palliative solutions. In order to achieve an elegant solution to clients' emotional problems, rational- emotive therapists need to employ not only cognitive techniques to dismantle their client's magical, empirically unvalidatable thinking but also a whole variety of behaviour modifying techniques, including role-playing, assertion training, desensitisation, operant conditioning and a number of emotive techniques such as shame-attacking exercises and humour. These methods are not used indiscriminately but within the RET theoretical framework.

THREE IMPORTANT RET INSIGHTS

There are three important RET insights in this framework which we will now outline.

Insight No 1.

Our self-defeating behaviour is related to antecedent and understandable causes. However, these antecedent events did not, by themselves, cause clients' problems, but rather clients' beliefs about the antecedent events or circumstances create these problems. As we teach our clients, "You feel as you think, and your feelings, your behaviour and your thinking are all inter-related. External events, such as being criticised or mistreated when you were young may have contributed to your emotional and subsequent behavioural reactions, but they did not cause your reactions. In the main, you create your own feelings by the way you think about and evaluate whatever you perceive is happening to you."

Insight No 2.

This is the understanding that regardless of how clients disturbed themselves in the past, they are **now** disturbed because they still believe the irrational ideas with which they created their disturbed feelings in the past and that they are still actively reindoctrinating themselves with these unsustainable beliefs, not because they were previously "conditioned" to hold these beliefs and now do so "automatically", but because they are continually reinforcing these ideas by their present inappropriate actions or inaction in addition to their unrealistic thinking. In other words it is clients' currently active self-propagandization that maintains their disturbed emotions and behaviour and enables these to hold sway over their life in the present. Until clients clearly accept responsibility for the continuation of these irrational beliefs, they are likely to make only feeble attemps to dispel them.

Insight No 3

This is the clear realisation and unflinching acknowledgement by clients that since it is their own human tendency to think crookedly that created emotional problems in the past, and that since these problems have persisted because of continued self-indoctrination in the present, there is nothing for it except hard work and practice if these irrational beliefs are to be uprooted and to remain uprooted until they wither to the point where they cease to be a problem. That means that repeated rethinking and disputing of irrational beliefs, together with repeated actions designed to undo them, are necessary if these beliefs are to be extinguished or minimised.

We conclude this section by briefly summarising the main points of RET personality theory:

(1) Human beings are born with a distinct proneness to create their own emotional disturbances, and furthermore, learn to exacerbate that proneness through social and cultural conditioning.

(2) Humans have the ability to clearly understand how they originally acquired and have continued to maintain their emotional and dysfunctional behaviour, and to train themselves to change or eliminate their self-defeating beliefs and habits.

(3) Self-reconditioning requires self-discipline (which humans can acquire) plus hard work and practice at understanding, contradicting and acting against their irrational and magical belief systems.

BASIC CONCEPTS: A BRIEF REVIEW

The main propositions of RET may be summarised thus:

(1) RET hypothesises that humans have a biologically-based tendency to think irrationally as well as a similar tendency to think rationally. On the one hand, we have powerful predispositions to preserve our lives, to seek pleasure and avoid pain, to use language, to think- often in highly creative ways, to organise our world, to love, to note and learn from our mistakes, and to actualise our potential for life and growth by experimenting with new individual lifestyles and social structures. On the other hand, we also have potent propensities to be self-destructive, hating, instant gratification seekers or short range hedonists, to shirk self-responsibility, to repeat our mistakes over and again, and to be dogmatic, grandiose, intolerant and superstitious.

(2) Our tendencies to think and behave in self-destructive or self-limiting ways are exacerbated by our culture in general, and by our family groups in particular. We are conditionable by social influences as well as by innate or biological tendencies. But we are at our most suggestible state when we are young, although we are gullible more or less throughout our lives. In short, we have distinct biosocial tendencies to act in one way or another, and in this respect each individual is unique.

(3) As noted above, we tend to perceive, think, feel and behave interactionally. It follows that to understand and eliminate self-defeating or disturbed conduct it is desirable to use a variety of cognitive, emotive and behaviour-modification methods within an overall conceptual framework. We call this framework the A-B-C model of human disturbance, and it is to this that we now turn our attention.

THE ABC MODEL

The ABC model of emotional disturbances is a quick and effective technique for conceptualising clients' emotional problems, and for helping them to identify and uproot the irrational components of their belief systems which are responsible for creating and sustaining their upsetting emotions and dysfunctional behaviours. Let's suppose that some obnoxious event happens to an individual at point A. We call this the Activating Event. Now, let's suppose that the individual (in this case male) feels emotionally upset at point C. Point C represents the consequences (s) that follow the Activating Event (A). Now, our individual convinces himself of two radically different things at point B, which stands for his belief systems. First, the individual convinces himself of an appropriate, or sane rational belief, namely: "I definitely don't like what has happened to me (at point A) and I wish it did not exist. But it has happened, there's no denying it. Tough!" If the individual stayed with that belief, how would he feel? He'd feel disappointed, sorrowful, irritated, or frustrated, rather than upset, disorganised or panicked. Why? Well, because realistically speaking, it is unfortuate that some unpleasant event has occurred and his appropriate feeling of annoyance may well motivate him to go back to the Activating Event at A and try to change it. Or if he can't change it, he can perhaps try to take steps to avoid it happening again in future. So, he may rationally acknowledge his feeling about what has happened, and if possible, try to do something about the problem situation. If the situation is one which cannot, for the time being, be changed, he can decide to lump it and learn how to figure out a way of avoiding a similar occurrence in future.

When, however, the individual feels upset at point C, he is telling himself something like, "I can't stand what has happened to me! It's **awful** that it exists, and it absolutely **shouldn't** exist! I'm a worthless Joe for not doing something to avoid it happening, and you are a louse for inflicting me with it!"

Can you see why this second set of beliefs is irrational? This second set of beliefs is irrational because

(1) it cannot be empirically validated or disproven, because it consists of magical assumptions;

(2) it leads to unpleasant emotional consequences which are quite unnecessary - for example, anxiety or depression; and

(3) instead of encouraging the individual to go back to the Activating Event at point A and try to change it (as his rational beliefs would), his irrational beliefs will interfere with and tend to block any constructive action he might be capable of taking, and may even help to make the situation worse.

Now let us analyse these irrational beliefs and see **why** they are unconfirmable. First, they represent a hypothesis that cannot be validated empirically. He **can** stand the unpleasant Activating Event at point A. He may never like it, and there is no reason why he should like it. But he **can stand,** he won't come apart at the seams!

(2) What does it mean to say that something is **awful**? How could one define it? It does not mean highly inconvenient or highly disadvantageous. Something more than that is implied. When applied to some stimulus, awful means more than 100% bad, more than 100% disadvantageous. But how can anything be more than 100% bad? Awful is a term carrying surplus meaning which has no definable empirical referent.

(3) Thirdly, by claiming that some unpleasant event in his life should not exist, the individual is issuing a God-like command that whatever he wants not to exist, absolutely should not exist. In effect, the individual is saying, "I am God, and I run the universe. So, what I say goes!" Obviously, this is another assertion that cannot be validated.

(4) Here, the individual thinks he is a worthless person because he failed to prevent the unfortunate Activating event from happening. Now, he is denigrating himself for his inability to order the universe to run the way he wants it. "I should be able to see that obnoxious things do not happen and because I failed to do what I absolutely **should** have done, that means I'm no good." In addition, by demanding that some other person must do his bidding and behave differ-

ently from the way they actually did behave, the individual again makes another useless and self- damaging assumption.

The basic tenet of RET, then, is that emotional disturbance is determined by the individual's irrational beliefs, and that these beliefs are irrational because they magically insist that some aspect or interpretation of the universe **should, ought** or **must** be different from the way it undoubtedly is. Although these irrational beliefs are connected with the Activating Events at point A, they bear no logical relation to these events. For they all boil down to the proposition, "Because I want something, it is not only desirable or preferable that it exists, but it **must** exist and it is awful when it doesn't!" No such proposition can ever be substantiated but, as therapists, you will come across literally myriads of people who devoutly cling to it, or to some equivalent variation of it. That being so, our previous assertion that humans are naturally crooked thinkers who find it easy to think in dogmatic, musturbatory ways, may no longer strike you as unusual.

To conclude this section, it is important to help clients to distinguish their **rational** beliefs about various Activating Events in their lives from their **irrational** beliefs, and to really understand why the difference is important. Help your clients to understand, until they need no prompting, that their inappropriate feelings stem from their strong dogmatic **shoulds, oughts** and **musts,** and that through challenging and uprooting these essentially magical notions they will be taking important steps to regaining emotional control over their lives. And if, at the same time, your clients work at, and practice acting against their deep-seated irrational behaviours, they can make headway against even their most stubborn self-defeating habits.

ACQUISITION AND PERPETUATION OF PSYCHOLOGICAL DISTURBANCE

Rational-emotive theory does not place much emphasis on an elaborate exposition of the way we acquire psychological disturbance. This is because of the rational-emotive view that we have a profound biological tendency to think irrationally. However, rational-emotive theory does acknowledge that environmental variables do contribute to our tendency to make ourselves disturbed by our own irrational belief system. Thus, if I am treated harshly by my parents I am more likely to make demands about myself and demands about uncomfortable life conditions than I would be if my parents treated me well. However, this is by no means always the case and we have come across people who have had "a harsh upbringing" but have made less demands about themselves, others and life conditions than do some of our clients who have had much more favourable upbringings. Thus, rational-emotive theory stresses that humans vary in their disturbability. The rational-emotive theory of acquisition can be encapsulated in the view that we as humans are not made disturbed simply be our experiences, rather we bring our ability to disturb ourselves to these experiences.

Rational-emotive theory does, however, put forward a more elaborate view on the ways humans perpetuate their own disturbances. First, as previously stated, it argues that humans perpetuate their disturbances because they lack three major insights:

(1) psychological disturbance is primarily determined by musturbatory irritation beliefs that people hold about themselves, others and the world;

(2) that people remain disturbed by reindoctrinating themselves in the present with these irrational beliefs; and

(3) that the only long-lasting way of overcoming disturbances is to work and practise against specific irrational beliefs and one's tendency to think and act irrationally.

RET theory contends that a major reason why we perpetuate our psychological problems is because we adhere to a philosophy of low frustration tolerance. Thus, we tend to be short range hedonists and to believe that we cannot stand discomfort, and even when we realise that we disturb ourselves with our beliefs in the present, we tend to think that just this awareness alone will lead us to overcoming our problems. Such individuals will do poorly in rational-emotive therapy and other forms of psychotherapy too, because they steadfastly refuse to make themselves relatively uncomfortable now so that they can be more comfortable later. In particular, they tend to procrastinate putting into practice outside their therapy sessions what they learn inside their therapy sessions and will frequently come up with a variety of "good excuses" why they didn't do their homework assignments.

A further way that clients perpetuate their own disturbances is because they make themselves disturbed (secondary disturbances) about their original disturbances. Thus, clients can make themselves anxious about their anxiety, guilty about their anger, depressed about their depression. ashamed about their own embarrassment etc., etc. Quite often, unless people tackle their secondary disturbances before their primary disturbances, they will impede themselves from overcoming their primary disturbances. Thus, unless a person accepts himself with his own anger problem instead of condemning himself for being angry, he will tend to get caught up in his self-blaming depression which will, in itself, stop him from dealing with his primary anger problem.

Rational-emotive therapists agree with their psychoanalytic colleagues that we frequently employ defences to ward off threat to our ego and to our level of comfort. This will lead us to tend to deny that we have psychological problems when we most definitely do and may lead to us blaming others or life conditions for our problem. Such clients tend to resist the hypothesis of rational-emotive therapy that they make **themselves** disturbed because if they were to admit this then they would, for example, severely condemn themselves. Unless the ideas that underlie their defensiveness are uncovered and dealt with, then little progress is possible.

We often perpetuate our own problems because we get some kind of pay-off from having such problems. Thus, we may get a lot of attention from others for having psychological problems which we are loath to do without, or our problems may protect us in our own minds from having more severe problems. When a person has a positive pay-off from having a psychological problem, such as attention from others, she is loath to work on overcoming her problems because she fears she may lose the attention which she craves from others. Here, note that in all probability she has an irrational belief about having such attention. When her psychological problem protects her in her own mind from a more severe problem then she will not be motivated to give up the emotional problem that she has at present, unless she is helped to also deal with the problem that she fears she might encounter.

Finally, we often perpetuate our own problems because we make self-fulfilling prophecies. Thus, a man who has difficulties trusting women may, when he meets a new woman, be quite suspicious of her and indirectly discourage her from having warm intimate feelings towards him. This may lead to her leaving him which would confirm in his mind that women were not to be trusted. Unless clients who make self-fulfilling prophecies are encouraged to see the contribution that they themselves make to these prophecies, they are likely to perpetuate their relationship problems in the future.

THEORY OF THERAPEUTIC CHANGE

The rational-emotive theory of therapeutic change is basically a simple one. It states that if clients are to overcome their emotional and behavioural problems, they need to

(a) recognise and acknowledge that they have a problem,

(b) overcome any secondary disturbance about the original problem,

(c) identify irrational beliefs that underpin the problem(s),

(d) understand why their irrational beliefs are, in fact, irrational, i.e., illogical, unable to be validated empirically, inconsistent with reality and will give them poor results in life,

(e) realise why uprooting their magical, unsupportable beliefs and replacing them with rational, realistic alternatives will give them more productive results,

(f) continue to challenge and dispute their irrational beliefs until they no longer carry conviction, and thereby strengthen their new rational philosophies,

(g) use a variety of cognitive, emotive, imaginal and behavioural assignments to strengthen their rational convictions and make them a fundamental part of their psychological make-up, as well as to seriously weaken their residual irrational notions,

(h) identify and overcome obstacles to therapeutic change using the same sequence as set out above, while still accepting themselves with their tendency to backslide and to construct such obstacles, and

(i) realise and act on the insight that, because they are fallible humans, they will, on occasion, slip back into irrational ways of thinking, but that they can fully accept themselves with that tendency and continue to work and practise against it for the rest of their lives so that it no longer seriously troubles them.

SUMMARY

Rational - Emotive Therapy is based on a clear-cut theory of emotional health and disturbance, and the various techniques it employs are used in the light of that theory, and not in a random, or hit or miss manner. Theory and technique are closely integrated at every stage of the treatment process. RET is hard- headed, scientific and empirically orientated and fosters the use of reason and the technology of emotional and behavioural re- education in the interests of human beings. RET is avowedly humanistic, existentialist and unashamedly hedonistic. It makes growth and happiness the central concern of our intrapersonal and interpersonal life and its efforts are devoted to that end.

CHAPTER FOUR

KEY PRACTICAL ELEMENTS OF RATIONAL-EMOTIVE THERAPY

In this chapter we will outline key elements in the practice of rational-emotive therapy.

Rational - Emotive Therapy is a structured problem-focussed approach to psychotherapy. Rational-emotive therapists help their clients to identify their basic emotional problems and to deal with them one by one in a structured and problem-focussed manner. Rational-emotive therapists consider their basic goal is to help their clients to identify the irrational beliefs that underpin their emotional disturbances and to challenge and change these beliefs in favour of rational beliefs. It is hypothesised that this will enable them to handle more constructively negative life situations and to lead more effective and fulfilling lives. RET can therefore be seen as an educational form of psychotherapy and the relationship between therapist and client is one of an encouraging teacher helping his or her students to grow by thinking for themselves. Thus, rational-emotive therapists favour adopting a Socratic-type dialogue with their clients in which the therapist encourages clients to question their own beliefs in an open-ended manner, but one which is directed to helping them to understand that while they cannot validate their irrational beliefs, they definitely can validate their rational ones. The aim of the rational-emotive therapist is to show clients how to accomplish this and teach them how to use the methods employed to solve their own emotional problems throughout the rest of their lives.

THE GOALS OF RET

RET therapists agree with their Adlerian colleagues on the therapeutic value of therapist encouragement. Their basic attitude towards their clients is that with hard work and effort they can change their irrational beliefs, replace them with more rational, realistic beliefs, and eventually help themselves to overcome their emotional and behavioural problems. However, the key aspect here is the hard work and practice which clients had better put in if change in their basic philosophy is to be anything more than "skin deep". Working consistently against their ingrained irrational philosophies in addition to acquiring more rational views of themselves and the world is of cardinal importance for clients in RET. Given their hard-headed scientific outlook on psychotherapy and the process of therapeutic change, RET therapists actively dissuade their clients from believing in quick, magical, painless and effortless cures. Instead, RET therapists show their clients that therapeutic change is certainly possible, but that it does require hard and concerted and sustained effort from clients. For this and other reasons, RET therapists encourage their clients to put up with personal discomfort and in certain ways encourage their clients to engage in challenging assignments, but not assignments that they would presently experience as overwhelming, in the service of therapeutic change.

Initially, rational-emotive therapists encourage their clients to identify their primary and secondary emotional and behavioural problems and to work on overcoming them. Ideally, however, rational-emotive therapists strive to enable their clients to make a profound philosphic change whereby they give up making demands on themselves, others and the world, and refrain from making exaggerated ratings of themselves and others. Clients are taught that while they may rate their deeds and performances, they cannot legitimately rate their "selves". The "self" is not a static entity but a process which undergoes frequent, or constant change throughout the life of the individual and therefore cannot be given any kind of global rating or score. The aim of such a profound philosophic change is to teach clients to accept themselves and others as fallible human beings, to habitually use the scientific method of testing their hypotheses about the beliefs they hold about themselves, others and the world, and by eliminating their dogmatic shoulds, oughts and musts, to minimally disturb themselves for the rest of their lives.

While this ideal focus on encouraging clients to make a profound philosophic change is important, rational-emotive therapists acknowledge that some clients may not be interested in making such a radical shift in their personality and they also recognise that many clients may not be able to embark on such a radical project. Thus, while rational-emotive therapists will offer clients an opportunity to embark on a more radical restructuring of their personality, they are flexible in adjusting their goals to meet the goals of their clients.

This flexibilty is also shown in their work with clients who are either unable or unwilling to work towards developing a new rational philosophy about specific elements of their lives. In such cases, rational-emotive therapists will alter their therapeutic goals and encourage clients to make changes in their interpretations, to work towards changing the negative events in their lives and to modify their behaviour so that they get some immediate benefit from the therapeutic process. However, rational-emotive therapists do recognise that for the most part such clients are vulnerable to future disturbance because they have not addressed the core of their emotional and behavioural problems, i.e., the musturbatory and dogmatic demands that they make about themselves, others and the world. Thus, rational- emotive therapists are willing to compromise and do not dogmatically insist that their clients always work towards addressing and overcoming their musturbatory cognitions.

Wherever possible, however, rational-emotive therapists strive to encourage their clients to internalise the three major RET insights that were outlined in the section on acquisition and perpetuation of psychological disturbance. To reiterate, rational-emotive therapists encourage their clients to acknowledge that past or present activating events do not cause their disturbed emotional and behavioural consequences; rather they strive to help their clients to acknowledge and internalise that it is their belief system about these activating events that "largely create their disturbed feelings and behaviours". Rational-emotive therapists also encourage their clients to believe that irrespective of how they have disturbed themselves in the past, they now upset themselves largely because they keep reindoctrinating themselves in the present with their irrational beliefs.

Finally, and most importantly, rational-emotive therapists strive to help their clients to see that because they are human and very easily, and to some degree naturally, tend to disturb themselves because they find it easy to cling to their self-defeating thoughts, feelings and actions, nevertheless, they can largely (but not totally) overcome their disturbances in the long run, mainly by working hard and repeatedly both to dispute their irrational beliefs and to counteract the effects of these beliefs by strongly acting against them.

THE THERAPIST-CLIENT RELATIONSHIP

Albert Ellis has argued that the role of effective RET therapists is akin to that of good teachers in that they strive to help their clients learn to become their own therapists once formal therapy sessions have ended. RET does not dogmatically insist that any one kind of therapeutic relationship between therapist and client be established; it thereby encourages therapeutic flexibility. Nevertheless, rational-emotive therapists do tend to favour establishing certain therapeutic conditions and therapeutic styles with their clients.

Therapeutic conditions

One of the most important goals of rational-emotive therapists is to encourage clients to unconditionally accept themselves as fallible human beings who often act self-defeatingly, but who are never essentially bad or good. As such, rational-emotive therapists themselves strive to unconditionally accept their clients in the same way and will strive never to put their clients down or to dogmatically insist that their clients must behave in certain ways. However, this does not mean that rational-emotive therapists would never bring to a client's attention aspects of the client's behaviour which are self- defeating and other-defeating. They thus strive to set up a therapeutic relationship where both therapist and client strive to accept themselves and the other person as fallible. The preferred rational-emotive therapeutic relationship, therefore, is an egalitarian one where both participants are equal in their humanity, although unequal at the outset with respect to skills and expertise in personal problem solving.

Partly because of the egalitarian nature of the therapeutic relationship, rational-emotive therapists strive to be as open as is therapeutically desirable and do not refrain from giving highly personal information about themselves should their clients ask for it, except when they judge that clients would use such information either against themselves or against their therapists. However, such openness and the self-disclosure which accompanies it are encouraged for ther-apeutic purposes. Thus, when rational-emotive therapists disclose that they have in the past experienced similar problems to their clients, it is not only to indicate that they are on an equal footing as humans with their clients but also to teach the clients how they, too, had to work to overcome these problems. Thus, in doing so, rational-emotive therapists serve as good encouraging role models. Here the basic message is "I am human too, I have experienced similar problems to you in the past. I overcame them and this is how I overcame them; perhaps we can look at my experience and you can learn from this experience and take elements of it and apply this to your own problem solving work."

Ellis has often noted that emotional disturbance incorporates the attitude of taking life too seriously and thus rational-emotive therapists tend to be ap-propriately humorous with most of their clients and will empathically and hu-morously demonstrate to their clients amusing aspects of the latter's dogmatic irrational beliefs and show them the therapeutic benefits of taking a serious but not overly serious attitude towards life. In doing so it is important to realise that this is done within the spirit of an unconditional acceptance of their clients and that such humorous interventions are directed not at the clients themselves, but at their self-defeating thoughts, feelings and actions. However, it should be noted that some clients do not benefit from such humour and thus the principle of therapeutic flexibility applies, namely, varying one's style of intervention to maximise therapeutic relationships with specific clients.

The world of psychotherapy has been heavily influenced by the work of Carl Rogers, in particular his statements concerning the importance of certain core therapeutic conditions, i.e., therapist empathy, genuineness and uncondi-tional positive regard. Rational-emotive therapists would agree with these, par-ticularly those concerning unconditional acceptance and genuineness. With respect to empathy, rational-emotive therapists not only believe in offering clients affective empathy, i.e., communicating that they understand how their clients feel, but also offering them philosophic empathy, i.e. showing them that they also understand the philosophies that underpin these feelings.

The one point where rational-emotive therapists would disagree with a large majority of therapists from other therapeutic orientations concerns the role of the therapist warmth in the counselling process. Rational-emotive therapists would argue that offering clients unconditional acceptance is likely to be of more importance than offering them undue counsellor warmth. For rational-emotive therapists the latter has two major risks. Firstly, therapist warmth may unwittingly reinforce their clients' dire need for love and approval, two irrational beliefs which rational-emotive therapists believe are at the core of much human disturbance. The second major risk concerns the fact that therapist warmth may also unwittingly reinforce the philosophy of low frustration tolerance that many clients already cling to. This is particularly the case if being warm means refraining from actively encouraging, and in some cases strongly pushing clients to involve themselves in uncomfortable experiences for the long term benefit of achieving therapeutic change.

Therapeutic style

Ellis (1979) recommends that rational-emotive therapists adopt an active directive style with most clients. He argues that such an active directive style, particularly at the beginning of psychotherapy, is important in that it encourages clients to very quickly and efficiently go to the philosophic core of their emotional and behavioural problems. However, effective rational-emotive therapists may vary their therapeutic style and adopt a variety of styles to fit the therapeutic requirements of different clients. Thus, they can adopt a formal therapeutic style with clients who believe that effective therapists are business-like and experts, and a more informal style with clients who would value interacting with a friendly personally involved psychotherapist; and, last but not least, a tough no-nonsense style with clients who would seem to benefit from such a therapeutic style. In addition, there may be indications for different therapeutic styles with clients with different personality styles. Thus, Beutler (1983) has argued that it is important to avoid developing an overly friendly emotionally charged style of interaction with "hysterical clients", an overly intellectual style with obsessive-compulsive clients and an overly directive style with clients whose sense of autonomy is easily threatened, as well as an overly active style with clients who very easily retreat into passivity. However, much more research is needed into this question of therapeutic flexibility with respect to counsellor style in rational-emotive counselling before any more definitive statements can be made on this issue.

It is important to realise, as will be shown in Chapter 5, that the relationship between therapist and client often changes during the process of rational-emotive therapy, but particularly with respect to the active-directive aspects of the therapist's style. Thus, when rational-emotive therapy is effective, therapists encourage their client to take on more responsibility for therapeutic change and consequently the therapist's level of directiveness fades. Here, rational-emotive therapists often take a less directive prompting role, encouraging their client to put into practice elements of the rational-emotive problem solving method which they will have increasingly gained experience in employing during the early and middle phases of counselling.

EMPHASIS ON DISPUTING IRRATIONAL BELIEFS

We argued in the theoretical section of chapter 3 that rational- emotive theory adheres to the principle of psychological interactionism, whereby it is held that beliefs, feelings and behaviours cannot be separated from one another, but in reality interact, often in quite complex ways. However, it is true that rational-emotive therapists direct much of their therapeutic attention to helping clients to dispute their irrational beliefs, cognitively, emotively, imaginally and behaviourally. This emphasis on disputing irrational beliefs involves first, the ability to detect the presence of these irrational beliefs; second, the ability to discriminate them from rational beliefs; and third, an ability to engage in a process called debating, whereby clients are encouraged to debate with themselves the illogical, unempirical and inefficient aspects of their irrational beliefs. However, it should be noticed that although cognitive disputing is a central component to rational-emotive therapy, it is by no means the only defining feature of this approach to psychotherapy. We wish to underscore this because many critics, and indeed many researchers who have carried out empirical studies of rational-emotive therapy, seem to equate RET with its cognitive restructuring aspects. Thus, while the central core of RET is teaching clients to dispute their irrational beliefs and to replace their irrational philosophies with rational philosophies, this is done in many different ways as will be shown below.

MULTIMODAL EMPHASIS

Rational-emotive therapists agree with multimodal therapists that it is important to take a multimodal approach to psychotherapy. Thus, rational-emotive therapists encourage their clients to use many cognitive, emotive/evocative, imaginal and behavioural assignments to encourage them to work towards changing their irrational ideas. In addition, because it stresses the biological as well as the environmental and social sources of human disturbance, rational-emotive therapists frequently favour the use of medication where appropriate, and physical techniques, including nutrition, exercise and relaxation techniques, as an adjunct to the therapeutic process. However, such methods are used to encourage clients to work towards changing their irrational philosophies and are not used necessarily as an end in themselves.

SELECTIVE ECLECTICISM

Rational-emotive therapy is what I *(WD)* have called a theoretically consistent approach to eclecticism (Dryden, 1987a). This means that rational-emotive therapists can and do use a wide range of therapeutic techniques originated by therapists from other therapeutic schools. However, in doing so they do not accept the theoretical principles advocated by these theorists from other orientations; rather techniques are freely borrowed from other schools with the major purpose of encouraging clients to identify, challenge and change their irrational beliefs. As such, it de-emphasises the use of methods which discourage or impede clients from adopting a direct focus on changing their irrational ideologies. Thus it avoids, although not in any absolute sense, using the following:

(a) procedures that help people become dependent, e.g., the creation of a transference neurosis and the use of therapist warmth as a strong reinforcer;

(b) procedures that encourage clients to become more gullible and suggestible, e.g., certain kinds of Pollyannish positive thinking methods;

(c) procedures that are long-winded and inefficient, e.g., free association and other psychoanalytic methods that discourage clients from focussing on their irrational beliefs;

(d) procedures that help people to feel better in the short term rather than to get better in the long term, e.g., some experiential techniques like getting in touch with and fully expressing one's feelings;

(e) procedures that have dubious validity and that have not received empirical support from research studies even though opponents claim great therapeutic success for these procedures (e.g., neurolinguistic programming); and

(f) procedures that include anti-scientific and mystical philosophies (e.g., faith healing and mysticism) and procedures that appear to be harmful to a variety of clients, e.g., encouraging clients as in primal therapy, to scream and shout and to explosively express their angry feelings.

It should be noted, however, that rational-emotive therapists may use some of these techniques for specific purposes. For example, using experiential techniques to help people to identify emotions prior to encouraging them to identify the irrational beliefs that underpin these emotions; using therapist warmth in the case of severe depression where the fact that a therapist may show that he is tremendously caring and concerned, may get through to such a depressed individual. In addition, Ellis (1985) has argued that he may even be prepared to use some of these inefficient techniques where all else fails with given clients.

THE IMPORTANCE OF HOMEWORK

Most rational-emotive therapists see their clients for one hour a week. Thus, they do not see their clients for the remaining 167 hours in the week. This is a salutary reminder to those who claim that what goes on within the therapy session is more important than what goes on between therapy sessions. Ellis has always argued right from RET's inception that clients who put into practice between sessions what they have learned within the sessions will do much better in therapy than clients who steadfastly refuse to act on what they have learnt in therapy. Thus, for rational-emotive therapists, encouraging clients to execute properly negotiated and well-designed homework assignments is considered to be a central part of the counselling process. Indeed, Ellis (1983) and Persons, Burns and Perloff (1988) have reported empirical data to suggest that clients who carry out homework assignments in cognitively orientated approaches to psychotherapy achieve a better outcome than clients who do not execute such assignments. Therefore effective rational-emotive therapists pay a lot of attention to the homework variable in therapy and spend sufficient time discussing why this is a central part of the therapeutic process with clients and devote sufficient time to adequately negotiating such assignments with their clients. In particular, they pay specific attention to factors which may discourage clients from successfully carrying out homework assignments and strive to troubleshoot such obstacles to psychotherapeutic change.

CONFRONTING AND OVERCOMING OBSTACLES TO CHANGE

We mentioned directly above that an important aspect of rational- emotive therapy is identifying and overcoming obstacles to therapeutic change that may arise when clients strive to execute homework assignments. However, obstacles to change pervade the entire therapy process and a feature of rational-emotive therapy is the recognition that such obstacles will occur and that a co-operative exploration between therapist and client concerning the nature of these obstacles, and the irrational beliefs that underpin them, is required as therapist and client attempt to overcome these obstacles so that they do not unduly interfere with the nature of therapeutic change. Obstacles to change can also occur within the therapy relationship; thus it may be that the particular match between therapist and client is not a good one and that the best way of handling this may be a judicious referral to a different rational-emotive therapist.

Also it has to be acknowledged that some clients do not find rational-emotive therapy a helpful therapeutic method and may well do better with a different approach to psychotherapy. This is because the ideas central to rational-emotive therapy, namely that one's emotional disturbance is determined by one's presently held irrational beliefs and the theory of therapeutic change, specifically, that one has to work and practice to overcome one's emotional and behavioural problems, are at variance with the beliefs of the client, and no amount of therapist intervention may change the client's mind on these points. Again, a judicious referral to a therapist from a different therapy school may be indicated. However, relationship obstacles to change can occur because the therapist has unwittingly adopted a therapeutic style which implicitly reinforces the client's difficulties. Thus, the therapist may be offering the client too much warmth and inadvertently reinforcing the client's needs for approval or the therapist may adopt an overly directive style of interaction which encourages an already passive client to become more passive in therapy and in life. It is important for therapists to monitor their style of participation and to continually ask themselves whether or not their therapeutic style is encouraging or discouraging their clients from changing.

The second source of obstacles to more lasting therapeutic change resides in clients themselves, and this issue of helping clients maintain their therapeutic gains will be dealt with in chapter 5. However, for present purposes it should be noticed that clients may have irrational beliefs about certain aspects of the rational-emotive therapy process which may discourage them from changing. In particular, they may well have a philosophy of low frustration tolerance towards taking major responsibility for effecting their own improvement. Thus, they may believe that they should not be expected to work hard in therapy and that doing so is too difficult and too uncomfortable. It is important that rational-emotive therapists encourage their clients to identify, challenge and change, such change-impending philosophies if clients are going to benefit in the long term from rational- emotive therapy.

Rational-emotive therapists are by no means immune from their own self-defeating beliefs which may well contribute to discouraging clients from changing. Thus, Ellis (1985) has outlined five major irrational beliefs that therapists may hold that may serve as obstacles to client change:

(1) I have to be successful with all of my clients practically all of the time.

(2) I must be an outstanding therapist, clearly better than other therapists that I know or hear about.

(3) I have to be greatly respected and loved by all my clients.

(4) Since I am doing my best and working so hard as a therapist, my clients should be equally hard working and responsible, should listen to me carefully and should always push themselves to change.

(5) Because I'm a person in my own right, I must be able to enjoy myself during therapy sessions and to use these sessions to solve my personal problems as much as to help my clients with their difficulties.

The presence of these beliefs may lead therapists to back off from encouraging clients to change when this is appropriate and desirable, or to become inappropriately involved with their clients in a manner that sidetracks rational-emotive therapy from its problem-solving focus. It is thus important for rational-emotive therapists to regularly monitor their work privately. They should be prepared to fully accept themselves if and when they discover that they are sidetracking the therapy process so that they can more effectively identify the irrational beliefs that underpin such sidetracking; and they had better consult frequently with their supervisors who may be able to spot sidetracking instances that they (the therapists) have not yet identified and which may indicate that their own irrational beliefs have come to the fore and are serving as an obstacle to client change.

FORCE AND ENERGY IN THERAPEUTIC CHANGE

The theory of RET holds that when clients are emotionally disturbed they tend to very forcefully and energetically cling to their main irrational beliefs, and that even when they have "insight" into these beliefs they may still strongly believe them and refuse to give them up. In such circumstances, rational- emotive therapists are not loathe to engage in very forceful and energetic disputing of their clients' irrationalities and to encourage their clients to intervene very forcefully, vividly and energetically when they are disputing their own irrational beliefs. Thus, force and energy can be brought to a whole host of cognitive, imaginal and behavioural assignments and serve to remind critics that rational-emotive therapy stresses the emotive aspects of psychotherapy and can bring passion to the counselling process. Indeed, rational-emotive therapists often encourage their clients to develop a passion for working forcefully and energetically to give up these beliefs,. Without this focus on force and energy, clients may well very weakly and insipidly challenge their irrational beliefs and will thus experience very little benefit.

No discussion of the key elements in RET practice would be complete without taking a look at what kinds of personality characteristics are associated with effective RET therapists. Since this important matter deserves a chapter to itself, the reader is referred to chapter seven.

In this chapter we have outlined the basic principles of rational-emotive therapy. In particular we have discussed the theory that underpins the practice of rational-emotive therapy and we have discussed the key elements of this approach to therapy in action.

CHAPTER FIVE

THE PROCESS OF CHANGE AND THE RET TREATMENT SEQUENCE

THE PROCESS OF CHANGE

We will now briefly outline a typical sequence in the process of rational-emotive therapy. At the beginning of therapy, therapists will encourage their clients to identify their major emotional problems and communicate their understanding of these problems from the clients' point of view. In the process of doing so, clients are helped to see that RET is a structured, problem-focussed approach to psychotherapy and personality change and one, moreover, which requires clients to work to achieve therapeutic change. Problems are taken one by one, and once clients have identified their problems, these are assessed with special reference to the irrational beliefs which the clients, with the aid of their therapists, have targeted for change. Therapists help their clients to question these beliefs and in later sessions to replace the irrational beliefs with more rational beliefs and to put these into practice to strengthen them and weaken their disturbance-creating irrational beliefs. Rational-emotive therapy rarely goes smoothly, and various obstacles to change do occur throughout the process. Here clients and therapists work together to identify such obstacles, and various modifications in therapeutic style, speed and focus are made as a result. In addition, clients' irrational beliefs about the process of therapy and about the process of change are targetted for discussion and change during this process.

THE RET TREATMENT SEQUENCE

We will now take you through the major steps of the rational- emotive treatment sequence and outline the 13 steps that we have identified as comprising this sequence.

Step 1: Ask for a problem

After you have greeted your client (in this case female), help her to discuss her reasons for coming for therapy, and to talk about her problems in a fairly open-ended manner, and show empathic understanding of her position. Then ask her for a specific problem to work on. This might be the client's major problem or the problem which she wishes to start on first.

Step 2: Define and agree the target problem

It is important for you and your client to have a common understanding of what this particular problem is, and a shared understanding that this problem will be the focus for initial therapeutic exploration. The more specifically you can help your client to identify the nature of the problem, the more likely it is that you will then be successful in carrying out an assessment of this problem. This is accomplished by using the ABC framework of RET, where A equals the activating event, or the client's inference about this event, B stands for the client's belief about the event, and C stands for the client's emotional and behavioural consequences of holding the belief at B. You can make this clear to the client by taking a specific example of her problem.

Step 3: Assess C

The first part of the RET treatment sequence involves the assessment of C, the client's emotions and behaviour. It is important at this stage that you help her to focus on an inappropriate negative emotion, such as anger, depression, anxiety or feelings of hurt, etc. You would also be advised to be on the look-out for self-defeating actions or behaviour, such as procrastination, addictions, and so on. However, clients who report experiencing concern, or sadness in response to a loss, annoyance or some other kind of disappointment, and who are taking effective action and leading self-disciplined lives, are in fact handling themselves constructively. This follows from the observation that it is generally regarded as unrealistic for human beings to have neutral or positive feelings about events in their lives. Thus, it is important at this point to help your client to identify a self-defeating neagative emotion, not a constructive negative emotion. At this step, you can also assess your client's motivation to change her inappropriate negative emotion and encourage her to strive towards experiencing the more constructive negative appropriate emotion. This, however, can be done elsewhere in the assessment part of the sequence (i.e., between steps 3 and 6).

Step 4 : Assess A

Once you have clarified what C is, you are now in a position to find out what your client specifically was disturbed about in the actual example you are assessing. If you recall from the Finger Pointing Exercise, the objective reality was that I *(WD)* was walking around the circle in front of the group, my hand raised in the air. That was the reality. Different workshop participants focussed on different aspects of the situation. Some of them, for example, focussed their attention on their own interpretations of the situation, such as that I was acting in an unfair manner. Others took the view that something threatening would happen as a result of my walking around in this manner. Consequently, it is important to realise that when you assess A, you are not only trying to assess the objective situation which your client was in, but the subjective aspects of that situation. This involves looking for your client's interpretations or inferences about A. Your major task here is to identify the most relevant interpretation or inference involved, the particular inference which triggered the client's emotional beliefs which in turn led to her disturbed feelings or behaviours at C.

Step 5: Determine the presence of secondary emotional problems and assess if necessary

It often transpires that clients have secondary emotional problems about their original emotional problems. For example, clients can often feel guilty about their anger, ashamed about their depression, anxious about their anxiety, guilty about their procrastination, etc. Therefore, at this point in the process, or earlier if appropriate, it is important to determine whether or not your client does have a secondary emotional problem about their primary emotional problem. If she does have a secondary problem, then it is important to target this problem for treatment first before proceeding to deal with the primary problem if you consider that the secondary problem is going to significantly interfere with your work on the primary problem. So, if your client is feeling ashamed about her anger, for example, then those feelings of shame may interfere with and possibly block effective work on helping her overcome her anger and thus shame (the secondary emotional problem) would be dealt with first in this case.

guilt ← anger

Step 6: Teach the B-C connection

Whether you are proceeding with your client's primary emotional problem or whether you have switched and are now in the process of assessing a secondary emotional problem, the next stage in the RET treatment sequence is to help the client to understand the connection between her emotions and her beliefs. Specifically strive to help your client to understand that her emotions do not stem from the activating event which she is discussing, or her interpretation of this event, but from her beliefs and evaluations about these events or interpretations. If you fail to do this, your client will be puzzled by your emphasis on assessing her irrational beliefs. It is important, therefore, to bring out the connection between the Bs and Cs at the right stage in the RET treatment sequence.

Step 7: Assess irrational beliefs

Assuming that you have successfully assessed A and C, you are now in a position to help your client to identify the particular irrational beliefs that she has about the event or situation that brought about her problem at C. In particular, be on the lookout for the following:

(a) *Demandingness*

Here your client will be making absolute demands about A in the form of 'musts', 'shoulds', 'oughts'. 'have to's', etc.

(b) *Awfulising*

Here, your client will be saying things like, "it's awful that A occurred, and that's terrible, or horrible."

(c) *Low Frustration Tolerance*

Help your client to look out for beliefs indicative of low frustration tolerance, or an attitude of "I can't stand it". Your client will frequently say something was intolerable, or unbearable, or too hard to put up with, etc.

(d) *Statements of damnation*

Under this heading you will hear your client making global negative evaluations of herself, other people and/or the life conditions she is living under. These global statements of evaluation can be extreme, such as, "I am a rotten person", or they may be less extreme but still basically irrational and unsupportable because they involve a total, or global evaluation of the self - which is, in reality, far too complex to be given a rating, or indeed, as you will see later, any kind of rating whatever. Thus, your client may, to use a less extreme example, insist that she is less worthy or less lovable as a result of what happened at A. This is still a global kind of rating, however, and if it occurs you will note it for later discussion.

Step 8: Connect irrational beliefs with C

Before proceeding to encourage your client to challenge her irrational beliefs, it is important, first of all, to help her see the connection between her irrational beliefs and her disturbed emotions and behaviours at point C. If this is not done, or not done adequately, your client will not understand why you will soon be proceeding to encourage her to question her irrational beliefs. Even if you discussed the general connection between B and C at Step 6, you still need to help your client to understand the specific connection between irrational beliefs and C at Step 8.

Step 9: Dispute irrational beliefs

The major goals of disputing at this point in the RET treatment process is to encourage your client to understand that her irrational beliefs are unproductive, that is, that they lead to self-defeating emotions which are illogical and inconsistent with reality. Moreover, these irrational beliefs cannot be supported by any factual evidence or scientific reasoning. By contrast, rational alternatives to these beliefs are productive, logical, consistent with reality and self-helping. They will not get the client into trouble, but instead, help her to achieve her goals in life with the minimum of emotional and behavioural upsets. More specifically, the goals of disputing are to help your client to understand the following:

(1) *Musts:* That there is no evidence in support of her absolute demands, while evidence does exist for her preferences.

(2) *Awfulising:* That what your client has defined as awful, that is, 100% bad, cannot be upheld and that in reality it will lie within a scale of badness from 0 - 99.9. Only one thing could be regarded as totally bad, and that is death itself; but even that is debatable since it is possible to regard death as preferable to dying slowly in excruciating agony with no hope whatever of relief. Often when you are helping your client to understand that if she rates something as 100% bad, she is really saying that nothing else in the world could possibly be worse. Once your client can see that this is absurd, she can more readily accept that her evaluation is greatly exaggerated.

(3) *Low frustration tolerance*: That your client can always stand what she thinks she can't stand, and can be reasonably happy, although not as happy as she would be if the difficult situation she has outlined at point A changed for the better.

(4) *Damnation or making global negative ratings of self, others or the world:* That this cannot legitimately be done because humans are human, that is, fallible beings, and are not in any way damnable no matter what they do or don't do. Further, human beings are too complex to be given a single global rating which completely summarises their total being. Statements like "I am worthless", for example, mean that I am totally without worth or value to myself or to anybody else and possess no redeeming features whatever. How could this ever be substantiated? Obviously, it couldn't. Similarly, the world, too, is not damnable and contains a mixture of good, bad and other complex aspects which cannot possibly be given some kind of a global rating. Once you can get your client to understand and accept this, she will become less inclined to deify or devilify herself or others and more able to accept herself and others as fallible, but non-damnable human beings.

At the end of Step 9, if you have been successful in helping your client to dispute her irrational beliefs, you will perceive a new awareness in your client of the lack of any real evidence to support her previously held irrational beliefs and an acceptance of these beliefs and evaluations as illogical and both self-and relationship-defeating. At the same time, you will observe the gradual emergence of the client's appreciation of why the new rational beliefs are logical, reality-based and self-helping, as well as potentially relationship-enhancing with others. A word of caution, however. Your client's newly acquired rational beliefs are unlikely to become deep, solid convictions overnight. She may say things like, "I understand what you are saying, and I think I believe it, but I don't feel it in my gut." It takes time for your client's new beliefs about herself and the world to sink in, so to speak, and to become an integral part of her psychological make-up. For that reason, the remaining steps in the RET treatment process are devised to help your client to internalise her rational beliefs to the point that she can say with conviction, "Yes, I now understand what you are saying in my gut as well as in my head and I can now act on this rational understanding".

Step 10: Prepare your client to deepen her conviction in her rational beliefs

At this point, before you encourage your client to put into practice her new learning, it is important to help her understand that long term therapeutic change does involve a good deal of hard work on her part if she is ever going to deepen her new rational convictions to the point that they become virtually a new rational philosophy of living.

Step 11: Encourage your client to put her learning into practice

You are now in a position to help your client put into practice a variety of cognitive, emotive, imagery and behavioural assignments. These are discussed with your client and she plays an active role in choosing assignments that are most relevant for her. At this point we would like to carry out two exercises to give you an opportunity to experience for yourselves what type of assignments are used in rational-emotive therapy. But for a fuller discussion of the variety of assignments that are used, consult Dryden (1987b) and Ellis and Dryden (1987).

RATIONAL-EMOTIVE IMAGERY

Rational-emotive imagery is an imagery exercise designed to help clients to gain practice at changing their inappropriate self- defeating negative emotions to more constructive negative emotions by changing their irrational beliefs to rational beliefs. Take one of your negative self-defeating emotions, such as anger, depression or feelings of hurt and vividly imagine the situation in which you experience these feelings. Close your eyes and clearly imagine the event in which you experienced those feelings and allow yourself to keenly feel the emotion concerned. Then, while still imagining the event as clearly and as vividly as you can, change your negative self-defeating emotion which is more constructive, but still negative. For example, if you are feeling angry, change that feeling to annoyance; if you are feeling depressed, change that to sadness; if anxious, change your anxiety to concern; and if you are feeling hurt, change your feeling of hurt to one of disappointment. Keep trying until you actually do change your self-defeating negative emotion to a constructive negative emotion.

Once you have succeeded, open your eyes and ask yourself exactly what beliefs you changed to bring about your change in feeling. Suppose you experienced anger; you would have changed that to annoyance by changing your irrational beliefs which created the anger. What were these beliefs? A fairly common one is, "The other person should not have treated me in that unfair manner, especially after all I've done for him!" If you changed your anger to annoyance, you probably told yourself something like, "While I don't like the other person's behaviour, there's no reason why he absolutely should not have treated me badly. I would much prefer the other person to treat me more considerately, and maybe I can persuade him to do so. But angrily damning him for his behaviour will only give me a pain in the gut and will probably induce him to be just as inconsiderate in the future! "

A different version of rational-emotive imagery involves you deliberately changing your beliefs while you are experiencing your self-defeating feeling in order to bring about a change in that feeling. Thus, vividly imagine the event in which you experienced your self-defeating negative feeling, identify your irrational demand(s) creating the feeling and deliberately change those demands to wishes or preferences, while still vividly imagining the event. If you were feeling anxious, for example, because you were demanding that a particular threatening event must not happen, continue imagining that the feared event might happen, but this time convince yourself that you would definitely prefer that the event didn't occur, but that there is no reason why it must not; and if it does occur, that might be unfortunate but it isn't terrible and you can stand it.

A SHAME ATTACKING EXERCISE

Shame attacking exercises are designed to help clients to act in what they consider to be a 'shameful manner' in public while gaining practice at accepting themselves for doing so but not putting themselves down for it. So, select some kind of behaviour, which if you performed in public would probably earn you scorn and lead you to experience shame for acting in that manner. However, make sure that your planned exercise is one which is unlikely to harm you or cause unnecessary alarm to others. We don't want you to land up in gaol, or lose your job! Some typical behaviours might be: wearing outlandish clothes which will attract the criticism of other people; acting in an inappropriate or inept manner in public, by going into a newsagent's shop, for example, and asking them if they sell bedroom suites; or asking a stranger for directions to the street along which you are actually walking. In other words, a shame attacking exercise involves socially inappropriate behaviour and the aim of the exercise is to show the participant that no matter how socially inept or foolish his or her behaviour may appear to others, they can still accept themselves in the face of public scorn or criticism without in any way downing themselves for their behaviour.

First look for the irrational belief behind the 'shame' of acting in the proposed manner; for example, the belief that other people will think you are something of an idiot and laugh at you and that you couldn't stand the disapproval of others. When you do your shame attacking exercise, it is important that you not only act in a socially inappropriate manner, but that you also at the same time dispute your irrational belief behind your feeling of shame. What are you telling yourself when someone notices your behaviour and either laughs at you, or tells you off? Is the criticism of others going to kill you, or is it merely unfortunate? Once you convince yourself that a foolish act cannot make you a foolish person but merely a person who acts foolishly, you can accept yourself as an imperfect human being who occasionally behaves stupidly or inappropriately but in no way is less worthy for doing so. Stay in the "shameful" situation until you have changed your feelings of shame to those of disappointment, irritation, or whatever other emotion is appropriate in the situation.

Step 12: Check the homework assignment

The next step in the RET treatment sequence is for you to check your client's reactions to doing the homework assignment you set. This may have been a shame attacking exercise, or some other activity which your client has been reluctant to face because of some emotional block arising from irrational beliefs concerning the situation. It is important to ascertain if she faced the situation that she agreed to face and whether or not she changed her irrational beliefs in the process of doing so. If the assignment was not carried out satisfactorily, reassign the task after verifying whether your client's failure was due to the continuing existence in her mind of those irrational beliefs and evaluations which the exercise was designed to undermine in the first place. Should that turn out to be the case, once more invite your client to identify and challenge the irrational beliefs which sidetracked her from carrying out the assigned task. When this has been done, reassign the task and monitor the result.

Step 13: Facilitate the working through process

Once your client has achieved a measure of success in changing some of her irrational beliefs by successfully executing the relevant homework assignments, go on from there to help your client to develop other assignments designed to help her gain experience in behaving in accordance with her emerging new rational philosophy. Thus, if your client has successfully challenged the irrational beliefs concerning public disapproval in social situations, help her to maximise her gains by designing assignments aimed at helping her to recognise and dispute any irrational beliefs she might have about disapproval in other situations such as work relations with colleagues or personal relations with significant others. Your aim is not only to help your client to recognise and rip up her irrational beliefs about whatever situation or problem is currently troubling her, but also to show her how to generalise her new learning to any future problem which she might experience. Once your client has gained experience and achieved success at challenging and disputing the irrational beliefs underlying one particular problem, she is more likely to take on greater responsibility for initiating the RET sequence with other problems. At the end of rational-emotive therapy, the degree of success achieved by both you and your client may be gauged by the extent to which she demonstrates the ability to live a more satisfying life with few, if any, of the emotional hangups with which she began therapy originally.

However even the brightest and most enthusiastic of clients may, on occasion, slip back into their old self-defeating ways. The answer? Back to the basics you go! It is on occasions like this, that you will see the emergence of what we referred to previously as secondary problems. Here, your client upsets herself because she has experienced some kind of a relapse. For example, your client may have felt guilty over some act of commission or omission and she is now denigrating herself for feeling guilty. "How stupid of me to upset myself again, and after all I've learned about RET! Boy, what a dumbo that makes me!"

If your client reports a relapse, consider it as normal, as par for the course. In any case, nobody is completely rational. We can think, feel and behave rationally most of the time and rarely upset ourselves over the various hassles and problems of living in a complex world. But can we realistically expect to be like that all of the time? Hardly! Assure your client, therefore, that to take two steps forward then one step back, is the common experience. Don't waste time commiserating with your client. Instead, repeat the 13 step RET sequence. Help your client to understand that staying emotionally healthy doesn't come about automatically, but requires continuous work and practice before the RET philosophy she has been trying hard to assimilate actually becomes an integral part of her life.

Show your client that there is no reason why she absolutely must not feel ashamed or dejected because some old emotional problem has returned to plague her. Encourage her to accept that this is normal, a natural part of our human fallibility. Emphasise (once more) that we all have innate tendencies to think in absolutistic, musturbatory ways and that we are all naturally crooked thinkers; it comes easy to us! At this point retrace your steps and use the ABC framework to re-orient your client back to the task of disputing her irrational beliefs. Your client already knows that her previous problem(s) became established through her habitually thinking thoughts that created it. OK. So, go after those irrational beliefs with your client. Get your client to identify, challenge and dispute them until she is thoroughly convinced of their falseness. Encourage her to look for variations of the main irrational beliefs and to understand **why** they are irrational and cannot be accepted as true, regardless of what form they are presented in. Help your client to keep looking, and looking, for her absolutistic demands upon herself and others, the **shoulds**, **oughts** and **musts**, and to replace them with flexible, non-dogmatic desires and preferences.

Finally, stress the importance, once more, of your client acting against her irrational beliefs until she becomes comfortable doing what she was already unrealistically afraid to try. Show your client how she can put muscle into her newly acquired RET philosophy by means of self-management techniques, rational-emotive imagery exercises and shame attacking exercises until she convinces herself that she really can make headway against even her most stubborn self-defeating beliefs and habits. When your client reaches the stage where she can easily recognise and distinguish her appropriate from her inappropriate feelings, understand why the difference is important, and demonstrate not only that she can uproot these shoulds, oughts and musts which underlie her inappropriate feelings, but also that she can replace these with rational beliefs, you may assume that your client is well on her way to regaining effective emotional control of her life.

CHAPTER SIX

SOME MISCONCEPTIONS ABOUT RATIONAL-EMOTIVE THERAPY

Whenever we have conducted workshops in rational-emotive therapy, workshop participants have made the following criticisms about RET. These tend to be misconceptions about this therapeutic method and we wish to outline and correct some of the more common of these.

(1) RET is Brainwashing

The idea that rational-emotive therapy is brainwashing is a misconception because RET therapists encourage their clients to think for themselves rather than telling them what to think. RET therapists adopt the Socratic method of challenging the core irrational philosophies their clients hold about themselves, other people, and the world that underly their problems. RET therapists encourage their clients to question their irrational beliefs for their own benefit and not for their therapists' benefit. RET therapists try to teach their clients the scientific method of logically examining their beliefs, to look for evidence in support of them, and to learn the difference between beliefs which are realistic and those which are unrealistic, illogical and irrational. They try to show their clients how thoughts, emotions and behaviour are all interrelated, and that the consequences of holding irrational, unsustainable beliefs are disturbed emotions and dysfunctional behaviours. RET therapists do not unequivocally tell clients that their irrational beliefs are inconsistent with reality, illogical and self-defeating. Instead, they try to teach their clients, through Socratic dialogue, how to apply the methods of science to their beliefs and see for themselves that some stoutly held beliefs are simply not viable, and therefore are largely unproductive or self-defeating in the long term.

(2) RET Therapists Tell Their Clients What to Feel and How To Act

This criticism is misconceived because, rather than tell their clients what their goals in life should be, RET therapists help them to identify their own basic goals and purposes. RET therapists assume that clients come to therapy in the first instance because they are not achieving their basic goals and because they have developed habitual dysfunctional behaviour patterns which keep getting them into trouble. For example, clients may repeatedly respond to both normal and unusual stimuli by over-reacting, or under-reacting emotionally, and may be quite unaware that their psychological problems arise from their misperceptions and mistaken ideas about what they perceive is happening to them. Even when they know that they are behaving poorly, clients will keep repeating non-adjustive or inappropriate responses to environmental situations. It follows that unless some inroads can be made into helping these clients change their self-defeating and maladaptive behaviours, their emotional and behavioural problems will persist, often with unfortunate consequences to themselves and to others. RET therapists help clients to identify their own idiosyncratic ways of enjoying life and, given that these are the clients' goals, help them to evaluate whether or not certain irrational beliefs that they cling to will aid or block them in the process of achieving their goals. Once the clients are in agreement that their irrational beliefs are sabotaging the realisation of their goals, then RET therapists demonstrate exactly how they can forthrightly question and challenge these beliefs, and induce them to work uproot these ideas and to replace them with scientifically testable hypotheses about self, other people and the world which are unlikely to get them into future emotional difficulties. This process is achieved again through the use of a Socratic dialogue where RET therapists encourage their clients to set their own feeling and behavioural goals and help them to maximise these through the use of rational thinking. It is not done by RET therapists unilaterally telling clients what they should feel or how they should act.

(3) RET is not Concerned with Clients' Emotions

Originally, Rational - Emotive Therapy was called Rational Therapy, but Ellis changed the name of the therapy to Rational - Emotive Therapy in response to critics' comments that RET therapists do not concern themselves with their clients' emotions. By now we hope you will have realised that RET is essentially, and fundamentally concerned with clients' emotions; indeed, the whole aim of the therapy is to help clients overcome their emotionl problems, and by recognising and uprooting the irrational cognitions underlying their problems, to help them to experience appropriate emotions in response to life's happenings, and to lead less frustrating and happier lives. RET holds that there are virtually no legitimate reasons why we need make ourselves emotionally disturbed about anything, but allows us full leeway to experience strong constructive negative emotions such as sorrow, regret, displeasure, annoyance and determination to change obnoxious social or environmental conditions. RET maintains, however, that when we experience certain self-defeating and inappropriate emotions (such as, guilt, depression, anxiety, worthlessness or rage), we are adding an unverifiable element to our rational view that some things in the world are bad and had better be changed. Moreover, so long as we cling to these negative, inappropriate emotions, our ability to change unpleasant conditions will be hindered, rather than helped. The essence of RET is that emotions are valuable - they motivate us to action, but we had better favour constructive, rather than destructive emotions if we are to survive happily in this world. And it is the hallmark of RET that we actually have enormous but not perfect control over our destructive emotions if we choose to work at changing the bigoted and unscientific notions which we employ to create them.

(4) RET is Just Concerned with Changing People's Beliefs

While we have outlined the key element of RET practice, and in fact focussed in this book on RET's distinctive features, RET therapists are also concerned with helping clients to change the negative events in their lives so that they gain more positive experiences. This frequently involves changing the negative activating events of their lives (the A's), and this is the best done, as argued above, by changing the irrational beliefs clients may hold about these events, and replacing them with reality-based convictions. When, however, negative events cannot, for the moment be changed, RET therapists will help clients to constructively adjust to these negative situations by encouraging them to change their thinking. Thus, if a male client is rejected after going for a job interview, the therapist will show the client that he can still accept himself, that the situation is unfortunate but not terrible, and that by refusing to down himself because of his failure to land a job this time, he can keep trying to find another job with a better chance of success than if he sat around and felt miserable. The therapist could even teach the client better interview skills. As we have stated above, appropriate negative emotions can be motivating. Consequently good RET therapists will encourage their clients to rid themselves of their irrational ideas which create those self-defeating negative emotions which tend to sabotage clients' efforts to achieve their goals. But good RET therapists will also encourage clients to take constructive action, learn more effective coping and other skills and to attempt to change negative life events.

(5) RET Encourages Clients to Become Unfeeling Robots

Nothing could be further from the truth! Indeed, RET is one of the few therapies which help clients to discriminate between their inappropriate and self-defeating negative emotions and their appropriate and constructive negative emotions. When clients are faced with negative life events, such as the loss of loved ones, RET therapists encourages such clients to keenly feel appropriate emotions such as sorrow, sadness and grief. An emotional-free existence, even if it could be achieved, has no place in the RET view of things. Such an existence would seem a very dull, sterile sort of state in which to "live" and could only be achieved by the abandonment of all desire and the creation of an attitude of total indifference to the world. That would be, indeed, the exact opposite of the RET philosophy, and no good RET therapist would ever attempt to do any such thing.

(6) A Consideration of Some Philosophical Objections to RET

(a) *How is a criterion of rationality determined?* This raises the question of who or what decides whether or not the client is being irrational, and that this contention is largely definitional. We can imagine some contending that the client is not irrational or disturbed, because he **should** be anxious or enraged and **should** actually enjoy these feelings or, others might argue that it is good for the client to be irrational since certain human values are enhanced by irrationality. We would agree therefore, that definitions of rationality and irrationality are somewhat arbitrary - in **any** of the main contemporary systems of therapy, and not just in RET. However, clients come to therapy because they, and not the therapist, think their life is not going well, and want help to change their ways and learn how to live a happier more self-fulfilling existence. In effect, clients come to therapy and say, "My way of doing things hasn't been working too well for me. Now, let's see if you can help me do better." This is then what RET therapists will help clients to do . Note, the definition that the clients' behaviour has been irrational and self-defeating up to this point is jointly accepted as such by client and therapist: the definition has not been thrust upon the client.

(b) *The idea that other people cannot affect you adversely.* This criticism contends that RET therapists encourage their clients to treat the responses of others as of little consequence and results in creating an illusion in the client of virtual impregnability to the world outside himself. In fact, RET therapists teach their client that other people can certainly affect them adversely in significant ways. Clients can be fired from their job, rejected in love, or ostracised for supporting unpopular social or political causes. However, RET therapists do try to help their clients to see the difference between being rejected by other people and rejecting oneself. We teach clients to see that their "ego" or self-regarding attitude **cannot** be adversely affected by others unless they take these others too seriously and by doing so give these others a power over their "self" that they otherwise do not have. In other words, when you are rejected, that doesn't necessarily make you a rejectee. You can refuse to allow your self-regarding attitude to be affected by others' positive or negative attitude towards you, while accepting that others have the power to harm or frustrate you as a human organism.

In conclusion, RET therapists encourage their clients to squarely face both direct and indirect threats to their well being. For example, RET therapists would agree with their clients that **concern** over hijacking, bomb threats, air pollution, political repression and racial injustice is legitimate and helpful in motivating people to change these things. But **overconcern** or panic is not constructive, and if clients can stop defining themselves as worthless individuals who cannot cope and if they can face these threats and difficulties with due concern, they will stand a much better chance of tackling them successfully.

CHAPTER SEVEN

PERSONALITY CHARACTERISTICS OF RET THERAPISTS

In my *(WD)* book with Albert Ellis *The Practice of Rational - Emotive Therapy* (Ellis & Dryden, 1987), we outline personal qualities of effective rational-emotive therapists what we have observed in our colleagues and in those trainees who seem to do well in practising RET. The more important of these qualities are listed below.

(1) Since RET is a fairly structured form of therapy, its effective practitioners are usually comfortable with structure, but flexible enough to work in a less structured manner when the need arises.

(2) RET practitioners tend to be intellectually, cognitively, or philosophically inclined and become attracted to RET because the approach provides them with opportunities to fully express this tendency.

(3) Since it is advocated that RET is often conducted in a strong, active-directive manner (Ellis, 1979), effective RET practitioners are usually comfortable operating in this mode, and are often skilled teachers and communicators. Nevertheless, they have the flexibility to modify their interpersonal style with clients so that they provide the optimum conditions to facilitate client change. For example, RET therapists often have a good sense of humour and use it appropriately in therapy but not with all clients.

(4) RET emphasises that it is important for clients to put their therapy-derived insights into practice in their everyday lives. Consequently, effective practitioners of RET are usually comfortable with using behavioural methods to facili-

tate client change, and with providing the active encouragement that clients often require if they are to follow through on homework assignments.

(5) Effective rational-emotive therapists tend to have little fear of failure themselves; this is because they do not invest their personal worth in bringing about their client's improvement; and because they do not need their clients' love/or approval. As such, and as noted later, they are not afraid of taking calculated risks if therapeutic impasses occur.

(6) Effective RET therapists tend to unconditionally accept both themselves and their clients as fallible human beings and are therefore tolerant of their own errors and the sometimes irresponsible acts of their clients. Effective RET therapists note their own errors and try to avoid making them in future with other clients, but do not condemn themselves for being error-prone. Practitioners of RET tend to have, or work persistently towards acquiring, a high level of frustration tolerance. This serves as a good model for clients to emulate and helps therapists to avoid feeling discouraged when their clients improve at a slower rate than desired.

(7) Effective RET practitioners tend to score highly on the following criteria of positive mental health and as such, serve as healthy role models for their clients.

(a) They practice enlighted self-interest in that they tend to be first and primarily interested in themselves and to put their own interest at least a little above the interests of others. However, they sacrifice themselves to some degree for those for whom they care but not overwhelmingly or completely.

(b) They also have a large measure of social interest, and they realise that if they do not act morally to protect the rights and abet social survival, it is unlikely that they will be helping to create the kind of world in which they themselves can live comfortably and happily.

(c) They are self-directed and assume personal responsibility for their lives while simultaneously preferring to cooperate with others. In doing so, they do not need the support or help of others although they regard these as being desirable.

(d) They are flexible in their thinking and are open to change. That is to say, they do not make rigid and absolutistic rules for themselves or others.

(e) They tend to have a high acceptance of uncertainty and do not demand that they must know what is going to happen to them or to others.

(f) They have a strong commitment to creative pursuits and they realise that they (and others) tend to be healthier and happier when they are virtually absorbed in something outside of themselves.

(g) They are successful in the application of scientific thinking to their own lives and in the practice of therapy. Such therapists tend to regulate their emotions and actions by reflecting on them and evaluating their consequences in terms of the extent to which they lead to the attainment of their short term and long term goals. Thus, effective RET therapists do not tend to be deeply religious, mystically minded or anti-intellectual in outlook.

(h) As noted above, effective RET therapists accept themselves as fallible human beings and can undefensively acknowledge making errors both within and outside of therapy. In unconditionally accepting themselves, they are less likely to continue making such errors than they would if they denigrated themselves for these errors. RET therapists accept themselves, note their errors, and patiently try to eliminate these errors or, at least, reduce the frequency of their incidence.

(i) They tend to take a fair number of risks and to try to do what they want to do even where there's a good chance that they might fail. They tend to be adventurous but not foolhardy.

(j) They tend to operate on the principle of long range hedonism and are willing to forgo short term pleasures when these interfere with the pursuit of their long term constructive goals. In this manner, too, they also serve as good role models for clients in that they demonstrate that instant gratification of desires may be counter-productive and may often frustrate the attainment of more important long term goals. In addition, RET therapists set an example of high frustration tolerance by showing that they do not have to get what they want immediately and can unrebelliously buckle down to doing necessary but boring tasks when it is in their best interests to do so promptly.

(k) They are non- Utopian in outlook and accept the fact that Utopias are probably unachievable. They also accept that it is unlikely that they will get everthing they want and that they will frequently experience frustration in their lives.

(l) They accept full responsibility for their own emotional disturbances and will strive to overcome their own emotional and behavioural problems by utilising the methods and techniques of RET. (In the final section of this book we will show how we have used the principles and methods of RET to overcome some of our own psychological problems.)

(m) Since RET advocates the use of techniques in a number of different therapeutic modalities (cognitive, imagery, emotive, behavioural and interpersonal) its effective practitioners are comfortable with a multi-modal approach to treatment and tend not to be people who like to stick rigidly to any one modality.

CHAPTER EIGHT

HOW WE USED RET TO OVERCOME OUR EMOTIONAL PROBLEMS

Windy Dryden:

When I was about four, I developed a stammer which led to a long and persistent period of teasing by my schoolmates in primary and secondary school. As a result, I began to view myself as a bit of a freak which, not surprisingly, hardly helped me to overcome my speech problem. I was taken (and in some instances dragged) to a variety of speech therapists over the ensuing years who uniformly failed to help me one iota with my stammer. I began to withdraw from talking in public, loathed speaking on the telephone and would literally quake with fear if anybody asked me my surname - which at the time was "Denbin"[1] since I would give a good impression of a machine gun being fired while trying to pronounce it. I did not have a clear idea of the "cause" of my anxiety, believing wrongly that the prospect of stammering was the main determinant rather than the "awfulness" of such a prospect. In my teens, I went to a local elocution teacher who taught me how to speak on the breath and this helped quite a bit, although I was still anxious about speaking in public. It was only when I reached my early twenties that I got my first real concrete help in overcoming my speech anxiety. This came when I saw Michael Bentine on television relating how he overcame his stammering problem. He told himself, "If I stammer, I stammer, too bad", or a similar variant. This seemed eminently sensible to me and I resolved to try this, albeit replacing his "too bad" with my more evocative "fuck it!" I simultaneously came to the conclusion that I had, up to that point, been defining myself as a "stammerer", which of course, was an over-generalisation. I

---

1   I changed my name from David Denbin to Windy Dryden mainly to avoid feelings of
    embarrassment concerning my difficulties in pronouncing "Denbin". I changed my first
    name to Windy because it was a nickname given me in my saxophone playing days, and
    because I liked it. Dryden was the name of our local telephone exchange.

undertook to re-define myself as a person who stammered at times, who spoke fluently at other times and who did a thousand and one other things, too. With these two cognitive techniques I helped myself to a great extent, particularly when I backed them up with a fair measure of in-vivo exposure. I literally forced myself to speak up in various social situations while reminding myself that I could tolerate the discomfort of doing so. All these techniques, I subsequently discovered, are frequently employed in RET. I had, at that time, not heard of psychotherapy let alone RET. Using these techniques, I have, to date, nicely stammered (and more frequently spoke fluently) in various countries without anxiety and can now speak for an hour on local radio without much apprehension and free from anxiety. I achieved this largely as a result of my own efforts (with help from my elocution teacher) and enjoyed the fact that I was the major source of my own improvement.

In the mid 1970's, I trained as a counsellor, being schooled mainly in client-centred and psychoanalytic approaches. I entered therapy, at that time, partly because I thought it was a good idea for a trainee counsellor to be in "personal therapy", but mainly because I was somewhat depressed. I had three relatively brief periods of psychoanalytic therapy with different practitioners. I found these experiences unhelpful in lifting my mood, was given no guidance on how to help myself and found most of the therapists' interventions puzzling , to say the least. One of my therapists slipped in, as it were, some psychodramatic techniques which helped me to "see" that my problem basically involved feelings of inadequacy. These were unfortunately traced back to my childhood which distracted me from solving my mood problem. I decided at the end of my third unsuccessful therapy that enough was enough and that I'd better help myself as best I could. I turned to Ellis and Harper's (1975) book - *A New Guide To Rational Living* because it stressed the use of self-help methods and because its content reminded me of my own successful efforts at overcoming my speech anxiety. I resolved to stop putting myself down, to accept myself as a fallible human being no matter what, and again pushed myself to do a number of things I wanted to do but was scared of doing because of the perceived threat to my "fragile ego". My depression lifted rather quickly and I began to feel more alive. All this without delving into my "sacred" childhood.

I remembered, at this time, that my clients had, from the beginning of my counselling career, asked for more specific help than I was providing them with through my reflections, clarifications and interpretations. I resolved to get trained in RET, believing then, as I do now, that it is important to be trained in counselling methods before using them with clients. This I did and I noted that (1) the large majority of my clients liked my new, more active-directive counselling approach, and (2) I felt more congruent practising RET. I seemed to have found my theoretical and practical counselling niche.

Since then, I have continued to use RET on myself. I have employed rational-emotive methods to overcome my anxiety about making an important career decision. I decided, as a result, to leave my full-time tenured academic position at Aston University, taking voluntary redundancy. Unfortunately, I overestimated my employability and was unemployed for two years during which time I coped with my new status with disappointment but did not make myself depressed. During this two year period I applied for and was rejected for 54 jobs or new positions. RET helped me in particular to overcome my anger about being turned down for re-training as a clinical psychologist. On being rejected, I began to believe such self-defeating ideas as "How dare they refuse ME. Who do they think they are? They should accept such a fine fellow and a scholar as myself and one with such good credentials to boot!" Noting that I was angry, I first accepted myself for needlessly angering myself and then disputed my irrational ideas. "Why shouldn't these people have their own (albeit, in my view, misguided) opinions which lead them to reject me?" The answer, in both cases, was the same: NO DAMNED REASON. I reminded myself that while I considered them to be wrong, they don't have to be right, and they are obviously right from their perspective. I'm still annoyed about their decisions whenever I think about it - but am not angry.

I have, thus, gained more therapeutic benefit from my own rational-emotive self-help methods than from formal therapy. Consequently I believe that my preferred therapy orientation - RET - reflects both my decided preference for helping myself in my own life and my view that therapists had better directly aid clients to help themselves in their lives. RET nicely succeeds, for me, in both respects.

Jack Gordon:

I would like to offer you another example of how RET was used to overcome a personal problem. In the process of doing so, I will use the material to draw out two important lessons which may stand you in good stead when you come to use RET, either on yourself, or when working on your clients' problems. Consider the problem of anger. First, it is important to recognise that anger can take several forms. Equally important is the recognition of the fact that anger can be used as a cover-up for something else. Take what is perhaps the commonest form of anger - "damning anger". Here you infer that some important goal has been frustrated, and that some person has broken a personal rule of behaviour deemed important in your personal domain. Your anger arises from your demanding that such frustrations of your goals and the transgression of an important rule of social or interpersonal behaviour absolutely should not have happened; and because it did happen, the individual responsible deserves condemnation and punishment for his or her damnable deed.

Another form of anger, which in RET is known as "angry hurt", arises when you infer that you have been treated "unfairly" and badly by some significant other, such as a spouse or lover. Let's say you have been "let down". You were promised something you had set great store on getting - a trip to Paris, a second honeymoon or something like that, and that lousy so-and-so of a boyfriend cancelled it and went off to a rugby international with his club friends. A typical reaction would be sobbing, shouting, feelings of "hurt". "You are no good for treating me like this. Damn your rugby match! You don't give a fig for my feelings. I never want to see you again!" The irrational belief here? It's quite clear: "I do not deserve to be treated like this, and I must not get what I do not deserve." There is also an element of damning anger in this response, but the main feeling of upset is one of "hurt". A common behavioural response in this situation is physical withdrawal from the person whose action precipitated the anger. If you can convince your clients that there is no guarantee that if they treat others kindly and considerately, others will respond in like measure, and if you can persuade them to give up the irrational idea that they must get what they think they deserve, and not get what they think they don't deserve, they will save themselves much needless unhappiness.

I can best illustrate a third form of anger by relating a personal experience I had a few years ago. This type of anger is called "ego-defensive anger" for reasons which will soon become clear to you. A woman friend with whom I had previously had a close relationship accused me one evening of not being sufficiently concerned about her health after she had undergone an illness. As we stood on the doorstep of her house she disparagingly compared my alleged lack of interest in her wellbeing with the concern expressed by her other friends after her return from hospital. Since I had not been invited round to see her and in fact had not been able to contact her for some time and therefore had no opportunity to find out about her state of health, I felt really "stung" by her, to me, "unfair" accusation of lack of interest. I still cared a great deal for her, although our relationship had changed, and I had helped her in various ways, and this accusation of implied indifference that came "out of the blue" was "the last straw" as it were. I foolishly blew my top, hurled angry words at her, slammed the door of her porch with an almighty bang and stormed off.

A preliminary analysis of this episode led to the conclusion that I had made myself angry when she implied that my behaviour towards her was evidence of a personal inadequacy. The presumed inadequacy was my failure to act towards her as a presumably loving person "should" act. Her implication was, "You say you love me, but you obviously don't!" If I acknowledged that she was right, or even if it was clear to me from her attitude that she thought that she was right, I would then have condemned myself for acting in a way I demanded I must never display. It is, of course, important that one's actions are in line with, or congruent with one's expressed feelings, especially where feelings of love or high regard are concerned. My woman friend appeared to be saying my actions were not in keeping with my expressed feelings. Thus, my anger served as a cover-up for my self-denigration or self-downing. But, why was I downing myself? What was essential about being seen by her at all times to be loving and attentive? What "terrible" thing might happen to me if she did not perceive me as loving and considerate of her feelings?

Shortly after storming off, I began to feel extremely miserable. I realised the "enormity" of what had happened; I had acted in my woman friends' eyes not only as someone who didn't care a damn about her, but had lost my temper

as well. I happen to be a person who very rarely feels angry. So here I was breaking another personal rule: losing my temper, and to her - of all people. She had
in her past relations with men suffered beatings, both physically and verbally,
and now here I was behaving towards her just as badly as some of her previous
bigoted, bullying men friends had. The result of all this self-downing was a
severe feeling of guilt. "How could I have been so damned stupid! I've blown
our relationship for good this time. How could I have done a rotten thing like
that - bawling her out when she wasn't feeling too well, and her of all people!
I'm obviously no better than those other so-called men who mistreated her in
the past. Now, she'll tell herself, "You men are all the same!" I really cursed and
damned myself until I felt really sick.

This is a good example of how anger can be used to cover up a threat to
one's "self-esteem". And the intense feeling of guilt and self-loathing which fol-
lowed so soon afterwards is also worth noting as a possible concomitant emotional disturbance which you may observe in similar cases (an example of a
secondary disturbance). It's certainly advisable to be on the lookout for it, for,
as we have pointed out, anger doesn't always appear alone.

First, I realised that anger was not the real problem, or at least, the major
problem. True, I had allowed myself to get angry over my friend's accusation
that I didn't care as much about her as her other friends apparently did. But
why did I anger myself over that? I had done the woman no harm. As it was, I
was staggered at her accusation that I didn't care; it was so totally unexpected.
And, it was also so unfair! Now, I was getting nearer! But I wasn't quite there
yet. Whether or not I had in fact treated my woman friend as inconsiderately as
she had implied was not the point; nor was it the fact that I considered her accusation "unfair". The basic question was, "Why is it so important, like a matter of life and death, that I have this woman's constant approval? Is it really true
that I can't possibly stand it if she thinks I'm a worm in spite of everything I've
done for her? It took a while before I was able to clearly see that I was putting
my "self" on the line, that I was making my self-acceptance or my personal worth
to myself dependent on whether this woman bestowed her approval on me. I
began to get it all together as I reminded myself that my intrinsic worth, or worth
to myself, is something that cannot be affected by other people's judgements or

standards. Some may like me, others may not. My worth or value to other people, - my extrinsic worth, may vary from person to person, depending on their own values and goals. But, my worth to myself is not up for sale. My worth to myself cannot be placed and weighed on some external measuring scale. As my feeling of worthlessness slowly dissipated, I began to vigorously challenge my other irrational ideas. Granted that it would be highly desirable to win back and retain this woman's love and approval, is it true that I absolutely must have it? If I fail to convince her of my feelings, and she rejects me outright, is that the end of the world? Do I really believe I have no future without her? Come now, do I really believe that? And could I never be happy again?

What rational beliefs eventually replaced the irrational beliefs with which I had made myself miserable? I eventually convinced myself that even if I had behaved in her eyes as badly as she implied that I had, that didn't in any way make me a rotten person, but only a person who, in this instance, had acted badly. I had not treated her badly in my eyes, but even if I had agreed with her appraisal, that in no way justified me belittling myself. "Alright, (I told myself), she might have made me a great partner, but do I absolutely have to act at all times in such a way that I dare not risk her disapproval, because if I do, I might lose her? No, I don't have to act at all times correctly and nicely, always looking over my shoulder to make sure she is not frowning at something I've done, or not done. I can treat her considerately like anyone else, but I don't have to bend over backwards just to hope I am pleasing her. If she can't accept me as I am, tough! I can always find someone else more suitable who will accept me as I am."

It was quite a battle. On the intellectual level, I was convinced by my own RET arguments. But at a deeper level I still wasn't sure! Now and again, my irrational "me" would say, "Yes, but suppose you are wrong about her. What if she really does care? Wouldn't it be terrible if you just assumed from her outward behaviour that she doesn't care about you and you went ahead and met someone else, and then discovered you could have won her back after all? She is just inhibited about expressing her real feelings, that's all." Such are the depths of self-deception you can experience when certain irrational ideas hold sway!

In the end, of course, RET won the day. The other important point I want you to pick up from this account is that intellectual insight alone isn't enough to bring about change. A client may say, as I did in the above example, "yes, I see the truth of what you're saying, BUT..." Whenever, your clients start "Yes, butting", be on the alert to do further work on disputing and to use other techniques if your clients are to make real headway against their ingrained irrational beliefs and dysfunctional habits.

As an addendum to my story of how I overcome my own problem, some time later, the same woman tried a little bit of emotional blackmail on me to get me to do her a favour. Her ploy was so patently obvious to me that I had to laugh. It didn't surprise me. I discovered that this woman had a low sense of "self-esteem" (as I, too, had then), and like other people who hold a similar view of themselves, tended to use various manipulative ploys to get people to go along with what she wanted, instead of coming out in the open and assertively ask others for their cooperation. It is easy to be wise after the event, but with hindsight, I now think my friend was trying to "wind me up" or emotionally blackmail me during the "doorstep" episode into doing some further favour for her that she had in mind. It came unstuck because she was quite shocked by my (unexpected) angry reaction. The point, of course, is that even if my diagnosis of her motives were true, her crooked motives were her problem, not mine. The point to remember is that you are responsible for the way the wheels go round in your head. If other people exhibit this or that symptom, that fact may be interesting and even useful in other ways, depending upon the nature of your interaction with them. But your emotional reaction is always your own responsibility. Regardless of their motives, other people cannot make you emotionally disturbed, unless you let them.

We hope that our personal experiences have illuminated your understanding of RET and that you can now see how you can use RET both practically with your clients and personally with yourself. Good luck on both counts.

BIBLIOGRAPHY

Beutler, L.E.(1983). *Eclectic psychotherapy: A systematic approach.* New York: Pergamon Press.

Dryden, W. (1984). Rational-emotive therapy. In W.Dryden (Ed.), *Individual therapy in Britain.* London: Harper & Row.

Dryden, W. (1987a). Theoretically consistent eclecticism: Humanising a computer "addict". In J.C. Norcross (Ed.), *Casebook of eclectic psychotherapy.* New York: Brunner/Mazel.

Dryden, W. (1987b). *Counselling individuals: The rational-emotive approach.* London: Taylor & Francis.

Ellis, A. (1962). *Reason and emotion in psychotherapy.* NewYork: Lyle Stuart.

Ellis, A. (1976). The biological basis of human irrationality. *Journal of Individual Psychology, 32,* 145-168.

Ellis, A. (1979). The practice of rational-emotive therapy. In A. Ellis & J.M. Whiteley (Eds.), *Theoretical and empirical foundations of rational-emotive therapy.* Montery, CA: Brooks/Cole.

Ellis,A. (1980). Rational-emotive therapy and cognitive behavior therapy: Similarities and differences. *Cognitive Therapy and Research, 4,* 325-340.

Ellis, A. (1983). Failures in rational-emotive therapy. In E.B. Foa & P.M.G. Emmelkamp (Eds.), *Failures in behavior therapy.* New York: Wiley.

Ellis, A. (1984). The essence of RET - 1984. *Journal of Rational - Emotive Therapy*, 2 (1), 19-25.

Ellis, A. (1985). *Overcoming resistance: Rational-emotive therapy with difficult clients*. New York: Springer

Ellis, A., & Dryden, W. (1987). *The practice of rational-emotive therapy*. New York: Springer.

Ellis, A., & Harper, R.A. (1975). *A new guide to rational living*. No. Hollywood, CA: Wilshire.

Kelly, G.A. (1955). *The psychology of personal constructs*. New York: Norton.

Persons, J.B., Burns, D.D., & Perloff, J.M.(1988). Predictors of dropout and outcome in cognitive therapy for depression in a private practice setting. *Cognitive Therapy and Research, 12,* 552-575.

RECOMMENDED READING

The following books written or edited by the authors of this book are rec-
ommended to those who wish to increase their knowledge of the theory and
practice of rational-emotive therapy.

(1) Dryden, W. (1987). *Counselling individuals: The rational- emotive approach.*
London: Taylor & Francis.

This book presents a clear and concise treatment manual for the practice
of rational-emotive therapy with individual clients.

(2) Dryden, W. (Ed.). (1990). *The essential Albert Ellis.* New York: Springer.

This book contains the most important articles published by Albert Ellis
on the theory and practice of rational-emotive therapy together with commen-
tary by the editor.

(3) Dryden, W., & Gordon, J. (1990). *Think your way to happiness.* London:
Sheldon Press.

This book is designed as a self-help book for clients as a supplement to
their therapy and for lay persons interested in applying the principles of RET
to their own emotional difficulties.

(4) Ellis, A., & Dryden, W. (1987). *The practice of rational- emotive therapy.* New
York: Springer.

This book shows how RET can be practised in a variety of treatment modalities including individual therapy, couples and family therapy, group therapy, sex therapy and marathons.

USEFUL NAMES AND ADDRESSES

(1) Institute for Rational-Emotive Therapy

45 East 65th Street, New York, New York 10021, U.S.A.

A comprehensive selection of books, tapes and videos and other materials on RET can be purchased from the Institute which also conducts training courses for those wishing to train in RET in the U.S.A

(2) IRET (UK)

c/o Al Raitt Ph.D.

13 Wellington Crescent,

Horfield, Bristol, BS7 8SZ. Tel. 0272:531110

Enquiries for training for RET in Britain should be sent to Dr. Raitt who is an Associate Fellow of the Institute for RET in New York and an accredited supervisor for training in RET.

Please enclose a stamped addressed envelope.

(3) Windy Dryden, Ph.D., is an Associate Fellow of the Institute for RET in New York and an accredited supervisor for training in RET. He has authored or edited 24 books and numerous journal articles and book chapters on RET, cognitive behaviour therapy and general psychotherapy. Dr. Dryden is a senior lecturer in psychology at Goldsmiths' College, University of London and a Chartered Psychologist and Fellow of the British Psychological Society. He is also in private practice as a RET therapist, and can be contacted at 14 Winchester Avenue, London NW6 7TU. Tel: 01: 624 0732.

(4) Jack Gordon, B.A. (Hons), is a lifetime student of RET, has co-authored two books with Dr. Dryden on Rational-Emotive Therapy and is currently a trainee RET therapist in private practice in Ruislip, Middlesex.

OTHER BOOKS IN THIS SERIES:

WHAT IS PSYCHOTHERAPY, A personal and practical guide, *Derek Gale, £4.95.*

ISBN 1 870258 01 0, 122pp.

The second edition of this popular book, updated and expanded! contains a very clear explanation of Freud's basic ideas as well as other areas of psychotherapy, especially Humanistic Psychology. Written after a series of workshops for would-be therapists, with practical exercises, checklists and roleplays.

WHAT IS PSYCHODRAMA, A personal and practical guide, *Derek Gale, £4.95.*

ISBN 1 870258 07 X, 100 pp. Publication Date: 28th April 1990.

The first British introduction to Psychodrama, a much used action therapy in groupwork, invented 60 years ago by J.L.Moreno. Derek Gale is well known for his Psychodrama Workshops; he writes in a very personal style, which makes the techniques easy to understand.

For full details write to:

GALE CENTRE PUBLICATIONS

WHITAKERS WAY

LOUGHTON, ESSEX

IG10 1SQ. Tel (01) 508 9344.